An Answer to Jura Populi Anglicani

AN

ANSWER

TO

Jura Populi Anglicani :

OR, THE

Subjects RIGHT

OF

Petitioning.

LONDON: Printed in the Year, 1703.
Price 1 *s.* 6 *d.*

THE
PREFACE.

THE Preface *that lets us into the Design of this piece of Malignancy, being too prolix for the Body of the Treatise, and of too great a Bulk for what is subsequent to it, I shall hold it unnecessary to give it the Reader* verbatim, *or answer it in the same method, that is,* Paragraph by Paragraph ; *but, by way of Abridgement, take notice of what is most remarkable in it.*

He begins with the dissatisfaction *which the Nation in general has entertrin'd against the* management of the House of Commons, *but more particularly their* Treatment of the Five Kentish Gentlemen : *when 'tis manifest from the reception which some of the Leading Members in that Affair have had in their several Counties and Burroughs, and the Universal Acclamations they have been welcom'd home with, that the People whom they represented had a grateful sense of the Services they had done 'em, and had been neither led away from their Duties by the sight of* Thom. Cockerill's *fine piece of* Sedition, *the* Kentish Petitioners Picture, *nor by 'Squire* Tate's *most elaborately dull Poem in praise of his thick-skull'd* Worthies.

But,

But becaufe the People are geneially known to ftand by the Acts of their Reprefentatives, (*which is a tacit Confeffion, that they ftand by what has lately been tranfacted, and contradicts the difpleafure of the Nation in general, which he pofitively affirm'd to* be burning hot *juft before)* be excufes himfelf, and makes an Intereft with them not to mifinterpret his meaning , for he does not reflect on the People in general, *but thofe particulai* Counties *and* Boroughs *that chofe thofe Gen'lemen who forwarded the Commitment of his mutinous Favourites , that is, the* Majoiity *of that Hcnourable Houfe. A fign indeed of a general Diffatisfaction, when he owns the* Electors *ftand up in Vindication of the* Elected, *which were known to be two thirds of the Members of Pai.ament , and certainly muft leffen the number of his Complainants*'

He brings it for an undoubted Maxim, (as furely it is) That if things are done contiary to Juftice and Reafon, the Majority of the Houfe does not give a Sanction to them , *which Negative includes this Affirm itive, That where Juftice and Reafon are the only Motives for a Vote or Refolution of the Houfe, there a Majority certainly ftamps an Authority upon it. But he either takes it for granted, and would have us do the fame, that thofe Worthy Members acted* contrary to Juftice and Reafon, *or knowing himfelf to be incapable of proving the Charge upon em, purpofely omits running into the Detail of that Injuftice, and keeps his Reafons for another opportunity.*

In another place he fays, Their Imprifonment was not an Act of the whole Houfe, *becaufe the*

honiteft

honeſteſt part of it, meaning thoſe that were of his Party, diſſented from it. Now in every *man's opinion, what is agreed to by a Majority of Voices in any Community or Society* f *Men whatſoever, is look'd upon as an Act of the whole, otherwiſe ſome peeviſh diſcontented Members, that have no great Inclination to the preſent Government, or the Church by Law eſtabliſh'd, might leſſen the Credit of Bills of Supply, by ſaying it was* no Act of the Houſe, *becauſe He voted againſt it, or that ſuch an Act of Parliament for the Preſervation of the Proteſtant Religion was of no Force, becauſe it had not* His Concurrence.

Next, he purſues the malignity of his Diſcourſe, by affirming, that the Houſe of Commons are not the whole People of *England*'s Repreſentatives, but only of thoſe who actually choſe 'em, *that* the Power Legiſlative is only Repreſentative in a Political State. *To make the Abſurdity of this Argument appear, and that they are eſteem'd otherwiſe, we need go no further than the form of Words which is generally made uſe of in all Impeachments, part of which run thus* : In the Name of the Commons, and all the Commons of *England*, &c *Now 'tis viſible from hence, that they themſelves think they repreſent* All *the Commons of* England, *otherwiſe they would not make uſe of their Names to impeach Offenders in, or thoſe who are look'd upon to be the moſt judicious part of the Nation are miſtaken in their Sentiments, which it is not Manners even ſo much as to ſuppoſe If the Legiſlative Power is their Repreſentative, certainly the Legiſlators themſelves may claim the ſame Title, ſince they are inveſted with that Power, and*
have

*have the exercife of that Authority which he gives
his decifion in favour of.*

*Another thing that feems (as he pretends) to dif-
courage him from the Profecution of the Difcourfe he
has fo manfully undertaken, is the* Judgment *people
will make of his* Intentions, *and the* Cenfure *that
probably will fall on him for defigning to ferve a*
Party, *and to let us into the knowledge of what he
means by the word* Party, *he gives us the Character of a* Tory *as given by himfelf, and the Principles of a* Whig *according to the definition of Men
of that Seditious Perfuafion Amongft the* Tories *he
intermixes a Lift of fome Worthy Members, as the
Speaker's Brother, &c and feems to make a wonder
why they, that were Men of the greateft* inveteracy *to the true* Tory Principles, *fhould be blended
with Sir* Edward Seymour, Sir *Chriftopher*
Mufgrave, *and others. I know not what he means
by* the true Tory Principles · *but if he ftands to
the Account he makes the Gentlemen of that Name
give of themfelves, it's what they need not be afham'd
of, efpecially when Men of direct contrary Principles ftand up in oppofition to 'em*

*However, at laft, tho' he feem'd unwilling to be
reckon'd a Scribe to a Party, he feems proud to own
that he cop es from St.* Paul *to the life, and, like a
true* Pharifee *which that holy Man was a Son of,
makes ufe of the Apoftle's words.* After the way
which they call Herefie, fo worfhips he the God
of his Fathers, *that is, makes an Idol of Sedition,
and* bows the knee to the Baal *of thofe that are
reftlefs and difcontented He needed not have made
this Confeffion, for a man would have guefs'd as
much from the Tide of his Book, and drawn an*

In-

Inference from his uneafinefs under Parliamentary Proceedings that he was a Lover of Anarchy *and* Confufion.

Nothing *more occurs in his Prefatory Declamation, befides his concern at the Bill againft the Tranflation of Bifhops, which he reflects upon Sir* John Packington *for, being to be fure a faft Friend to the Bifhop of* Worcefter, *whofe many Tranflations from one See to another it feems to fquint at, and the good Bp. of* S--ry's *acquaintance, who has all manner of reafon to think the Diocefe of* Winchefter *better than his own, and who deferves the higheft Preferment in the Church as much as he does what he is* now poffefs'd of. *Why he fhould be fo zealous for Epifcopacy, 'tis not in my fphere to imagin, unlefs he ftands np for that Holy Order by way of oppofition, or why he falls upon the Lower Houfe of Convocation, unlefs he would fhew himfelf a profefs'd Enemy to all Clergy-men who will not be rid upon.   He was for the Liberty of the Lay-men juft before; but would have the inferiour Clergy, which are the moft Exemplary Men for their Learning and pious Converfation of all that wear that holy Garment, have no manner of Privileges; which fhews, that he's for having a Power affum'd over all People but Men in his own ftation, and even is refolv'd to maintain hard and faft, that the Lords fhould exercife a Defpotick Authority over thofe that reprefent the Nation, even to fuch a defpicable Partizan as he is: when what* Memmius *fays in his Oration to the People of* Rome *concerning the Exorbitancy of Power ufurp'd by the Nobility, may be adapted to our purpofe, and may ferve as a fort of remembrance to that Venerable Affembly*

Aſſembly which has lately ſo honourably aſſerted its *Rights and Privileges* Superioribus Annis taci- ti indignabamini Ærarium expilari, Populos Liberos paucis Nobilibus Vectigal pendere, penes eoſdem & ſummam Gloriam, & maxi- mas Divitias eſſe tamen hæc talia Facinoia impune fuſcepiſſe parum habuere Itaque po- ſtremo Leges, Majeſtas veſtia, Divina & Hu- mana omnia hoſtibus tradita ſunt, *&c.* At qui ſunt hi qui Rempublicam occupavere ? Ho- mines ſceleratiſſimi, cruentis manibus, imma- ni avaritia, nocentiſſimi idemque ſuperbiſſimi, quibus *Fides, Decus, Pietas, poſtremo honeſta atq,* *inhoneſta omnia quæſtui ſunt. What ſort of Grie-* *vances this Orator hinted at, may be ſeen in the* *Hiſtory of* thoſe, *and whom theſe Complaints are* *apply'd to, may be known from the Conſtitution of* *the* preſent *Times ſo that there needs no other* *Explanation but that the* Commons *of* England *would have been in the ſame Condition, were it* *not for the prudent Reſolves of our* preſent Se- nate.

Jura

Jura Populi Anglicani
ANSWER'D,
Paragraph by Paragraph.

THE Death of the King of *Spain,* and the alteration made in the Affairs of *Europe* by the Settlement of his Dominions, has cau-fed a general Confternation in all thofe Countries which before had any apprehenfions of Danger from the growing Power of *France* Among them all, none has more reafon to be alarm'd than *England,* fince, when we confider our Scituation, the Affairs of Commerce and Rel'gion, and the Inte-reft not only of the Abdicated Family, but of their great Protector likewife, among us we muft al-low that no other Nation (unlefs perhaps we will except *Holland)* is more immediately affected, and likelier to feel the firft dire effects of this unhap-py Conjunction

This the People of *England* are generally fen-fible of, and 'tis to this fenfe of their Danger, and the fufpicion they have entertain'd of a much grea-ter inclination to continue than deftroy this Union of Power, that we are to afcribe their Difcontents, and the Refentments they have expreffed againft their Reprefentatives, to a degree never before known in any Age of our Government.

B   'Twas

'Twas in the midſt of theſe Clamours that ec-
cho'd through the Kingdom, and the univerſal diſ-
ſatisfaction of the People at the Proceedings of the
Houſe of Commons, that the five Kentiſh Gentlemen preſented this following Petition, agreed to
by the Gentlemen, Juſtices of Peace, Grand Jury,
and other Freeholders, at the General Quarter-
Seſſions holden at *Maidſtone*, the 29th of *April*, in
the 13th year of his Majeſty's Reign.

" WE the Gentlemen, Juſtices of the Peace,
" Grand-Jury, and other Freeholders, at the
" General Quarter-Seſſions at *Maidſtone* in *Kent*,
" deeply concern'd at the dangerous Eſtate of this
" Kingdom, and of all *Europe*, and conſidering
" that the Fate of us and our Poſterity depends up-
" on the Wiſdom of our Repreſentatives in Parlia-
" ment, think our ſelves bound in duty humbly to
" lay, before this honourable Houſe the conſequence
" in this conjuncture, of your ſpeedy Reſolutions,
" and moſt ſincere Endeavours to anſwer the Great
" Truſt repoſed in you by your Country
" And in regard, that from the experience of all
" Ages, it is manifeſt no Nation can be happy with-
" out Union, we hope that no pretence whatſo-
" ever ſhall be able to create a Miſunderſtanding
" between our ſelves, or the leaſt diſtruſt of his
" Majeſty, whoſe Great Actions for this Nation
" are writ in the Hearts of his Subjects, and can
" never, without the blackeſt Ingratitude, be for-
" got
" We moſt humbly implore this Honourable
" Houſe to have regard to the Voice of the People,
" that our Religion and Safety may be effectually
" provided for , that your Loyal Addreſſes may
" be turn'd into Bills of Supply, and that his moſt
" Sacred Majeſty (whoſe propitious and unble-
" miſh'd Reign over us we pray God long to con-
" tinue)

" tinue) may be enabled powerfully to affift his Al-
" lies before it be too late.

And your Petitioners fhall ever pray, &c.

*Signed by all the Deputy-Lieutenants there pre-
fent, above twenty Juftices of the Peace, all
the Grand-Jury, and other Freeholders then
there.*

Anfwer. *There is no perfon in his fenfes but will
grant, that the* Spanifh *Succeffion, according to the
Settlement made in his late* Catholick Majefty's Will,
has alter'd the Ballance of Europe, *and aggrandiz'd
the Family of* Bourbon *to an extraordinary degree of
Power · but no Inference is to be drawn from thence
that* We *are oblig'd inftantly to have recourfe to Arms,
who are no Parties concerned in the faid Will, who
have no Right or Title to the leaft fpot of Ground belonging to the Kingdoms bequeath'd in it, and who have
enter'd into fuch a perpetual Peace with* France *and*
Spain, *that cannot be violated without a manifeft
breach of Faith on the fide of the Aggreffor Our Scituation indeed, the difference of Religion, which they
call* Herefie, *and the Intereft the late King and his
Family has in the neareft of thofe Kingdoms, may entitle us to fome Jealoufies and Apprehenfions of his
moft Chriftian Majefty's Defigns, and make us provide
againft any Emergencies whatfoever, as far as the impoverifh'd ftate of the Nation will allow, and the weak
condition of our Pockets, which have groan'd under the
preffures of a long and expenfive War, are capable to
permit but that a People fhould be diffatisfied with
their Reprefentatives that ftudy'd the Confervation of
the Peace, fhould enter into Clubs and Confederacies,
and run canvaffing after Subfcriptions to difturb the
publick Tranquility, which has fo lately been fecur'd to
'em by the Treaty of* Refwick, *is a plain Indication that
the perfons who bufie themfelves in fuch Impertinencies*

take

take *Meafures that are unjuftifiable for their Impru-
dence. and deferve more than a* Gatehoufe-*Punifhment for the Prefumption that bears it Company. As
for the* Petition, *the Judgment which has been paffed
already upon it, and the Voice of that Venerable Affembly which declar'd it* Scandalous, Infolent, and Seditious, *has, I queftion not, fuch an Authority with thofe
that have not bid adieu to their Underftandings, as to
render it of a very difagreeable and tumultuous Complexion, and if Inferiours, who have invefted Superi-
ours with the defence of their Rights and Privileges,
and have refign'd every thing as it were to their difpo-
fal (as to thofe who are the beft Judges of what is moft
advifable for 'em) take upon 'em to give Advice to their
Councellors, as they prefcribe* Bills of Supplies *inftead
of* Loyal Addreffes, *they ought to be reminded of their
Duty by fuch Punifhments as may deter others from the
like Arrogances* The Subject, *fays Sir* Humphrey
Mackworth *in his judicious Treatife*, has an undoubted Right to petition the Lord Chancellor ,
but not to give his Lordfhip any affront and if he
fhould prefume in fuch a Petition to defire the Lord
Chancellor *to turn his plaufible Speeches into juft and
righteous Decrees*, I prefume his Lordfhip might
commit him to the *Fleet* for fuch an Indignity to
the Court.

Jura Pop. Ang

This Petition was offer'd to the Houfe on the
8th day of *May* , the Gentlemen who deliver'd it,
and own'd it at the Bar of the Houfe, were Mr.
William Colepepper, Mr. *Thomas* Colepepper, Mr *David* Polhill, Mr *Juftinian Champneys*, and Mr *William Hamilton* , for fo I find all their Names written in the Votes, without the addition of *Efq*, tho'
four of them were Juftices of the Peace, and two
Deputy-Lieutenants of the County This was
thought by fome to be prudently contriv'd to leffen the Credit of the Petition among People without doors, and to make others lefs eager to follow
the

the Example of thofe Gentlemen. Concerning the Petition the Houfe came to this Refolution, That 'twas *Scandalous, Infolent and Seditious, tending to deftroy the Conftitution of Parliament, and to fubvert the eftablifhed Government of this Realm* The five Gentlemen they order'd to be taken into the Cufto-dy of a Serjeant at Arms The Treatment they had from him was very fingular, and fhew'd that they were under the high difpleafure of the Houfe, for when he accidentally faw two of them talk to-gether, he drew his Sword upon his Deputy for permitting it, and when upon one of thofe Gen-tlemen's demanding a Copy of their Commitment (which they reckon'd they had a Title to, by vir-tue of the *Habeas Corpus* Act) and his refufing it, the Gentleman faid, he hop'd the Law would do him Juftice his Reply was, that *he car'd not a fart for the Law* The Reverence of the Law is fallen very low indeed, when one who has the Honour of be-ing a Servant to the Houfe of Commons can pre-fume to make fo bold with it. In his Cuftody they continu'd till the 13th of *May*, when he (contrary likewife to the *Habeas Corpus* Act) by an Order of the Houfe of Commons, and a Warrant iffu'd out from the Speaker, deliver'd them Prifoners to his Majefty s Prifon at the *Gatehoufe,* where they con-tinu'd to the end of the Seffion. Befides this fevere Punifhment inflicted by themfelves, that they might fhew their utmoft Refentment, and pro-ceed to all the Severities in their Power, they at the fame time refolv'd upon an Addrefs to his Ma-jefty to put them out of the Commiffions of the *Peace* and *Lieutenancy*

Anfw *The omiffion of the Title of* Efq, *it feems fticks mightily in the Gentleman's ftomach, becaufe four of 'em were Juftices of the Peace, and two Deputy-Lieu-tenants when the very Orders of the Houfe, as may be feen in the printed Votes, very feldom give that fo-norous Appellation to their own Members, but run thus.*

Order'd,

Order'd, That M^r such-a-one carry the Bill to the Lords, &c *But the Engraver that gave us their Seditious Effigies has pleas'd 'em to the life, in not only cutting* 'Squire Colepepper, &c. *but has given 'em their Coats of Arms into the bargain. The Serjeant at Arms for his part is known to be a Gentleman of singular Humanity, and if he is obliged to make use of some things that may look like Severities, it is for fear of disobliging the Members of that House whose Servant he is, and whom it is his Interest to keep a good understanding with, in his valuable Post, And Mr.* Powell's *respect for the* Laws, *as well as the* Legislators, *is so great, that he utterly denies any other Reflection on it, than that when one of the five Mutineers threaten'd him with a Prosecution, he gave him to understand, but in more decent Terms, that he defied him, since he was under the Protection of that high Power which would stand by him in the Execution of his Office*

The Imprisoning of those Gentlemen is the Fact which comes under my consideration. In order to handle this Subject fully, 'twill be necessary that I consider these things. *First*, What Power the House of Commons has to imprison. *Secondly*, The Subject's Right of Petitioning *Thirdly*, What Reasons the Gentlemen, Justices of the Peace, and Grand-Jury of the County of *Kent*, had to offer that Petition when they did

First, I am to consider what Power the House of Commons has to imprison. Tho' this enquiry may by some be thought needless in this place, since a bare setting forth the Subject's Right to petition will be sufficient to shew us what we are to think of the imprisoning of the *Kentish* Petitioners; yet the best way, I think, to enable us to make the truest Judgment concerning this Fact, will be to examine what Provision the Laws have made for the Liberty of our Persons, and how far we are subject to the Will of the House of Commons.
Such

Such an enquiry would be highly neceſſary at this time, tho' the treatment of the *Kentiſh* Petitioners had given no occaſion for it Great Numbers of other Subjects have been impriſon'd by them this Seſſion, to the horror and amazement of all thoſe who know the Rights and Liberties of the People of *England*, and therefore cannot but be concern'd to ſee them ſo miſerably infring'd. To prevent ſuch Acts of Power for the future, 'tis neceſſary that we ſhew that they are meer Acts of Power, and manifeſt Incroachments on the Liberties and Rights of the People If there be any who ſtill re-tain the old fond Opinion they had of the Peoples Repreſentatives, and think that our Liberties are ſufficiently provided for when they are in the hands of ſuch Guardians, and that we can ſuffer no great Inconvenience by any Power which they are entruſted with, I would deſire them to enquire how Mr. *Buckley* (committed for ſhewing the Let-ters which he received from Sir *Edw-d Sey---r* and Mr. *Colſon*) and Mr. *Haſſam* (committed on Mr. *Samuel Shepherd*'s Account) were treated by the Ser-jeant at Arms in their Confinement, and conſider whether ſuch Severities are not ſufficient to con-vince them, that the Peoples Repreſentatives (as they are call'd) are not to be complemented with more Power over the Liberties of the People, than our Laws and Conſtitution do allow them ? Do not the fierce and rigorous Proſecutions which we have ſeen make it evident to us, that Men can fall under no Reſentment, no Rage, or Malice, more outrageous than that of a Party ? Don't we ſee how regardleſs Men can be of their Reputati-on, what little and unbecoming Artifices they can ſtoop to, when they are intent upon breaking an oppoſite Faction ? Is it fit then that in ſuch a diſ-orderly and divided State, Men ſhould be entruſt-ed with exceſſive Power, who are inclin'd to make ſo ill uſe of it ? If by our Conſtitution the Houſe

of

of Commons were allow'd a Power to reſtrain the
Freedom of our Perſons, as they ſhould think fit,
for the good of the Community, the exerciſe of
that Power, however rigorous and ſevere, would
(if it were free from the biaſs and influence of Parties) be as patiently born from them, as any other
hands whatſoever. But if by a Lawleſs and Arbitrary Power they invade that Freedom which an excellent Conſtitution entitles us to, 'tis impoſſible
that a regard for the Perſons who afflict us ſhould
reconcile us to the Suffering 'Tis my buſineſs
here to diſcover whether they have done ſo, or
no The propereſt method to do this, and to ſa-
tisfie this firſt enquiry concerning their Power to
impriſon, will be, Firſt, to examine how far our
Laws have ſecured the Liberty and Freedom of
our Perſons Secondly, to examine whether the
Power exercis'd by the Commons be not repugnant to the Laws, and plainly deſtructive of our
Conſtitution.

Anſw. *The Method that our Author promiſes to
take in Vindication of thoſe* Gentlemen, *he ſhould by
all means call* Squires, *on account of their high Poſts,
has all imaginable appearance of what is fair in it,
and his Orthodox way of dividing the Text into three
Parts has been ſo long approv'd from our Pulpits, that
no Exceptions can be made againſt it But we may
make an eſtimate of his deſigns to ſtate the Caſe, and
in whoſe favour he intends to decide the buſineſs in
hand, from the little Artifices he makes uſe of in relation to Sir* Edward Seymour's *Letter, and the Treatment of the* righteous and plain dealing Mr. Shepherd's *Agent He tells us, Mr.* Buckly *and Mr* Haſſam
*were hardly us'd, the fiſt committed on account of ve-
ry indecent Reflections on an Honourable Member of
the Houſe, which is a Breach of the Privileges of Parliament, the laſt for his concurrence with indirect practices, and forwarding the great Concern of Bribery,
which was in agitation amongſt ſome perſons who have*
                                                        been

*been expell'd the Houfe, but he would inftance in the
particulars, were there any Truth in his Allegations,
he lays down in fuch general Terms   If they had a fevere Treatment, 'twas the juft Refult of their Crimes,
and thofe Perfons who are now at Liberty, ought to
thank the Houfe that they did not make ufe of further
Severities, fince the Law directs Punifhments beyond
Imprifonments in Cafes of Bribery, and orders a ple-
nary Redrefs for falfe Accufations   What is hinted
at further in this Paragraph is fo much of a Pe,ce
with what is gone before, that it will be unneceffary to
dwell any longer upon it, wherefore let us look into
his two Subdivifions, in relation to the Common and
Statute Law.*

As to the firft enquiry, 'tis evident that both
the *Common* and *Statute Law*, of this Land, as they
fuppofe Men to have an Inheritance in the Liberty of their Perfons, fo have they taken all imaginable care to fecure them in the Poffeffion of this
Inheritance

1ft, As to the *Common Law*, we know what
favour fhe fhews to the Liberty of our Perfons.
This was fo great, that formerly fhe fuffered none
to be imprifon'd, but for Force, and things done
againft the Peace.   Force indeed fhe (being the
Guardian and Preferver of the Land) could not but
abhor, thofe therefore that committed it, fhe accounted her Capital Enemies, and did fubject
their Bodies to Imprifonment   In all other cafes
fhe protected them from this Reftraint   This
was our Conftitution in the time of the *Saxon*
Kings, and a long while after, till the 35th year
of *Hen* 3d, who was the eighth King from the
Conqueft   Becaufe Bailiffs would not render Accounts to their Lords, 'twas then enacted by the
Statute of *Marlebridg*, cap 24, that their Bodies
fhould be attach'd   Had this Law been a little
unreafonable, 'tis no great wonder that it fhould
pafs at that time, confidering the weaknefs of the

C   King

King, and the Power of the Lords, in whoſe favour 'twas made. We may remark concerning
it, that the firſt Act to reſtrain the Subjects Liberty was procured by thoſe Lords who forced a
Charter from the King to confirm their own Liberties Three Reigns after this (23 Edw 3 17)
becauſe Men took no care to pay their Debts,
'twas provided by another Statute that their Bo
dies ſhould be attach'd. Before theſe Statutes, as
I ſaid, no Man's Body was ſubject to be taken or
impriſon'd otherwiſe than as aforeſaid As the
Moderation of our Anceſtors in not enacting any
ſuch Laws, in all the Ages that went before, de-
monſtrates the great regard they had for Liberty ,
ſo did the Courſe and Practice of the Law afterwards fully ſhew how great a Puniſhment they
reckoned to have it reſtrain'd, as by thoſe Statutes Before the Reign of K James I 'twas allow'd, that he who died in Priſon diſcharged the
Debt, how great ſoever it was, for which he was
committed The reaſon was, becauſe they
thought Impriſonment a Puniſhment ſo great, that
no other ſatisfaction ought to be demanded after
it 'Twas the opinion they had of the greatneſs
of the Puniſhment,that made our merciful Forefa-
thers bear with Men in uſing ſuch Acts of Force to
enlarge themſelves, as are not now allow'd The
Statute de frangentibus Priſonam, made in the firſt
year of Edward the Second, enacts that no one
ſhall undergo Judgment of Life or Members, for breaking of Priſon alone, unleſs the Cauſe for which the
Perſon is impriſon'd require ſuch a Judgment And
the Mirrour of Juſtices, which was writ before
this King's Reign, where it reckons up the Abu
ſions of the Common Law, tells us, That 'tis an
Abuſe to hold an Eſcape out of Priſon, or the Breach
of the Goal, to be a mortal Offence, FOR AS MUCH
As ONE IS WARRANTED TO DO IT By THE
LAW OF NATURE All this cannot be won
der'd

der'd at, when we confider how great an evil
Imprifonment is reckon'd, and that 'tis in Law
called *Civil Death Perdit Domum, Familiam, Vi-
cinos, Patriam, he lofes his Houfe, his Family, his
Wife, his Children, his Neighbours, his Country, and
is condemned to live among wretched and wicked Men.*
For this reafon it is that as a Man, if he be threatned to be kill d, may avoid a Feoment, Gift of
Goods, *&c* So it is, if he be threatned to be imprifoned, or kept in Durefs, that being reckoned
to be a Civil Death, any Specialty or Obligation, made by him is null in Law And he
may avoid the Action brought upon fuch Specialty, by pleading that it was made by Durefs
Anfwer,

*The Common Law, it muft be confefs'd, fhews great
favour to the Liberties of our Perfons, but certainly it
has regard to what is Equitable and Juft, and if Perfons formerly were Imprifon'd on Account of making
ufe of force, or threatning to make ufe of it, or any o-
ther Breach of the Peace, he has brought an Argument
againft himfelf which Juftifies the Confinement of the
5* Kentifh *Gentlemen, fince the Law allows, that coming in a Tumultuous manner with Petitions, getting
Subfcriptions through a whole County to Affront the
higheft Courts of Judicature, is a direct Breach of the
Peace None of 'em being Imprifon'd for Debt, it is
needlefs to fearch into the Statute of* Edward *the* 3 d
*or for him to Quote it, but it is plain if the Gentleman
that writes this practices the Law, he may have Clients
enough if he can clear PoorDebtors from anyObligations
from Bonds which have been fign'd and deliver'd in
Prifons*

As the *Common Law* has fhewn a great regard, fo
fecondly has the *Statute Law* of this Land abundant-
ly provided for the *Liberties* of our Perfons This
is evident from many Acts of Parliament The
firft that I fhall take notice of is the *Grand Charter* of the Liberties of *England* granted firft in the

(12)

17th year of K *John*, and renewed twice in the Reign of King *Henry* the Third. By that Charter it is provided that *no Freeman shall be taken or imprison'd, unless it be by Judgment of his Peers, or by the Laws of the Land* That is, by *Jurors* who are his *Peers* , or by due *Process of Law* That this is the meaning of thofe Words *per Legem terræ*, or *Law of the Land*, will plainly appear from divers other Statutes wich explain thofe Words In the 25 *Ed.* 3 c 4. we find them thus explained in thefe Words *Whereas it is contain-ed in the Great Charter of the Franchifes of* England, *that no Freemen be imprifon'd, or put out of his Freehold, nor of his Franchife, nor Free Cuftom, unlefs it be by the LAW OF THE LAND, it is accorded, affented, and eftablifh'd, that from henceforth none fhall be taken by Petition or Suggeftion made unto our Lord the King, or to his Council, unlefs it be by Indictment or Prefentment of his good and lawful People, of the fame Neighbourhood where fuch Deed was done, in due manner, or BY PROCESS MADE BY WRIT ORIGINAL AT THE COMMON LAW, and that none be out of his Franchifes or Freehold, unlefs he be duly brought in to anfwer, and fore-judg'd of the fame by COURSE OF LAW And if any thing be done againft the fame, it fhall be redrefs'd and held for null* The 28th of *Edw* 3 is very direct to this purpofe There 'tis enacted, *That no Man of what Eftate or Condition he be, fhall be put out of his Lands or Tenements, nor taken nor impri-fon'd, &c without he be brought in to anfwer by due PROCESS OF LAW* 36 *Ed* 3 *Rot Parl Num* 9 Amongft the Petitions of the Commons, one of them, being tranflated out of *French* into *Englifh*, is thus, *Firft, That the Great Charter, and the Charter of the Foreft and the other Statutes made in his Time, and the Time of his Progenitors, for the Profit of him and his Commonwealth, be well and firm-ly kept and put in Execution, without putting Diftur-*

bance

*bance, or making Arreſt, contrary to them, by ſpecial
Command, or in any other.* The Anſwer to this Petition, which makes it an Act of Parliament, is,
*Our Lord the King by the Aſſent of the Prelates, Dukes,
Earls, Barons, and the Commonalty, hath ordain'd and
eſtabliſh'd that the ſaid Charters and Statutes be held
and put in Execution according to the ſaid Petition ;
which is, that no Arreſt ſhould be made contrary to the
Statutes by ſpecial Command*

This explains the matter fully, and is of as
great force as if it were printed , for the *Parl.
Roll* is the true Warrant of an Act, and many are
omitted out of the Books that are extant.

36 Ed 3 Rot Parl. Num 30 explains it further , for there the Petition is, *Whereas it is con-
tained in the Grand Charter, and other Statutes, that
none be taken or impriſon'd by ſpecial Command, without Indictment, or other due Proceſs to be made by
Law* , yet oftentimes it hath been and ſtill is, that many are hindred, taken and impriſon'd without IN-
DICTMENT, or OTHER PROCESS to be
made BY THE LAW upon them as well of things done
out of the Forreſt of the King, as for other things :
That it would therefore pleaſe our ſaid Lord to command thoſe to be deliver'd who are taken by ſpecial
Command, againſt the Form of the Charters and Statutes aforeſaid* The Anſwer is, *The King is pleas'd
if any Man find himſelf griev'd, that he come and make
his Complaint, and Right ſhall be done unto him* 37
Edw 3 c 18. agreeth in Subſtance, when it ſaith,
*Though it be contain'd in the Grand Charter, that no
Man be impriſon'd, nor put out of his Freehold without
Proceſs , nevertheleſs divers People make falſe Suggeſtions to the King himſelf, as well for Malice as o-
therwiſe, whereat the King is often griev'd, and divers
in the Realm put in Damage, againſt the Form of the
ſaid Charter · wherefore 'tis order'd that all they who
make ſuch Suggeſtions, be ſent with the Suggeſtions before the Chancellor, Treaſurer, and the Grand Council,*

ana

*and that they there find Surety to purfue their Suggefti-
ons, and incur the fame pain that the other fhould have
had, (if he were attainted) in cafe that their Suggefti-
ons be found evil, and that then Procefs of the Law be
made againft them without being taken aud imprifon'd
againft the Form of the faid Charter and other Statutes.* Here the Law of the Land in the *Great
Charter* is explain'd to be *Procefs of the Law.*

Anfwer,

*As his Quotations from the Common-Law might
have been left out, as bearing no relation to the Subject in hand, fo he might have forborn the Recital of
the Statute-Law The great Charter, and feveral Acts
of Parliaments in diverfe King's Reigns fince King
*John's *Time provided for the Liberty of the Subjects
(viz) That they fhould not le imprifon'd without
Procefs, or Indictment, but many fubfequent Statute
fince their time to forward a due Execution of Juftice
have taken care likewife of the Priviledges of our Supe
riors, as in the Reigns of their late Majefties* Charles
and James *the 2 d as alfo in thofe of* Henry *the 7th
and 8th as may be feen likewife in the Parliament
Rolls For if Criminals were not imprifoned, and by
clofe Confinement forc'd to appear and anfwer to their
Indictments, what would become of the Law, and how
large would be the Number of Offenders If a Scandalous and defamatory Perfon, a Man that whifpers a
bout Jealoufies and groundlefs Sufpicions thro' the Na
tion, and vilifies the Magiftracy muft have his Liber
ty till he can be brought to a Formal Tryal, without
doubt we fhould be to feek for the Malefactor at the
day appointed for hearing his Offences ? The wifdom of
the Nation has therefore taken care for the bringing
fuch Delinquents to Juftice, tho' fometimes as in the
Cafe of the* Kentifh Petitioners, *the mercy of our Supe
riors has been fuch, as to content themfelves with de
priving 'em for fome time of their Liberty, when the
might have order'd them to be profecuted after the
breaking up of the Seffion, and this Power of Imprifon
                                                    ing*

ing Perfons that are not Members has been exercis'd and claim'd as an undoubted Right in the Commons in all former Reigns, and has been made ufe of thro' the whole Courfe of his prefent Majefty's, and never interrupted or attempted againft till this very time, when Faction is grown barefac'd, and Malecontents dare fhew themfelves in Print, and fhed their Venome in Publick Places.

From what I have here delivered, it appears what care both the *Common* and *Statute Law* have taken of the *Liberty* of our *Perfons*, that the former abhor'd Imprifonment, and never allow'd it, unlefs it was when Men had been guilty of *Force*, and render'd themfelves Enemies to the Community, and that the latter has frequently enjoin'd that it fhall not be inflicted, unlefs it be by *Indictment*, or fuch *due Procefs* as the Law requires What we have here faid will affift us in

Anfwer,

What he has here deliver'd (*in the words of the Preacher*) *has nothing to do with the Cafe of Perfons whofe defence he has undertaken, fince any Intelligent Creature knows that Riotous Affemblies as getting of hands by way of Remonftrance againft Parliamentary Proceedings, imply a fort of threatning, to make ufe of force if they did not comply without it , and Sir* Edward Seymour's *faying,that the Petition fmelt of* Forty One *was veryAppofite to the Papers.fince the Proceedings in thofe days came to fuch a high head from the very fame beginnings*

The fecond thing propos'd, which was to enquire whether the Power exercis'd by the *Houfe* of *Commons* be not an Invafion of our Legal Rights, and tends not to fubvert even our Conftitutions ? The Laws are called (*Edw* 6 *Fol.* 36) *The great Inheritance, and the Inheritance of Inheritances, without which a man can have no Inheritance.* The greateft Inheritance a Man hath is the Liberty of his Perfon, for all others are neceffary and

fubfervient

fubfervient to it   If then the *H - fe* of *Com———ns*
have invaded that fundamental Liberty of our
Perfons, which by *Magna Charta*, and feveral o-
ther Statutes, as well as the moft ancient Cuftoms
and Laws of this Land, we are entitul'd to, this
will inform us how far the Powers exercis'd by
them have deftroy'd our Legal Rights. *Magna
Charta* fays, that *no Freeman fhall be taken or im
prifon'd, but by the Judgment of his Peers, or th*
Law of the Land But 'tis certain that Men imprifon'd by them underwent no Judgment of their
Peers, were not committed by legal Procefs or by
any Law that we know in this Land. I know 'twill
be faid, that by the Words of *Magna Charta* we are
to underftand not *legal Procefs*, but the *Law of the
Land* generally, and that the Words extend to
all the Laws in the Realm   Since then there are
Laws and Cuftoms in Parliament, and by thofe
Cuftoms Imprifonment is allow'd, 'twill be faid
in favour of the *Houfe* of *Commons*, that they in
committing People do not neceffarily deftroy that
Right which we have by *Magna Charta*   'Tis
true, there are Rules and Cuftoms in Parliament,
and by thofe Cuftoms they have a Power to imprifon   But that is a Power which extends to their
own Members , fuch a Power is neceffary within
their Society, becaufe without it 'twould be impoffible to keep the Members of it to fuch Rules
and Orders as muft neceffarily be obferved by
fo great a Body of Men, engaged in fo weighty
and important Bufinefs   Confinement here is no
violation of the Right Men have to the Liberty
of their Perfons by *Magna Charta* , that Right
they all give up, and fubmit to the Rules of the
Houfe, when they make themfelves Members of
it. It muft be confeffed that this Power has
been extended farther to Perfons who are not
Members, as in cafes of breach of Privilege, and
Contempt. I fhall not here take notice of the
rife

rife of this Power, and how great a Grievance
the exercife of it has been to the People of this
Land, but muft obferve, that in a Liberty has
been taken of confining thofe who offer'd violence
to *Members* in their own Perfons, or in their Servants or Eftate, becaufe fuch Moleftations, if allow'd, might give them too great difturbance,
and ruin the Bufinefs of the Publick, yet it muft
not from hence be inferr'd that the *Houfe* of *Commons* has an abfolute or an unlimited Power to
imprifon whom, and for what caufe they pleafe
If there are fome Confinements order'd by that
Houfe, which are not, 'tis fure there may be fome
which are repugnant to *Magna Charta*, otherwife
Magna Charta, and all the other Acts which
defigned to fecure our Liberties from the Invafi-
ons of our Kings, whofe Subjects we are, and to
whom we owe Allegiance, have left us expos'd to
the Arbitrary Will of our *Fellow Commoners*, who
(thanks be to God) have yet no fuch Rule or
Dominion over us

Anfwer,

'*Tis certain, thofe that are the Peoples Reprefinta-
tives affert the Peoples Rights as they ftand up for
their own, fince their Priviledges are infeparab'e, and
that the five Prifoners beforemention'd, were legaly
committed fince they receiv'd their* Mittimus *from
the Fountain of Law from whence all Commitments
proceed, and if ev'ry private Juftice of the Peace can
fend Criminals, or at leaft thofe who are reputed to
be fo, to Goal, certainly, Gentlemen in fuch Publick
Stations as the Members of the Houfe of Commons may
be invefted with as high an Authority The Magiftrate
he orders 'em to be kept in hold, in order to fecure 'em
to ftand Tryal, and certainly they that make the Magiftrate, in the Perfon of the Supream Magiftrate,
even the Kings moft Excellent Majefty can have the
fame Prerogative over the People, and it no more
deftroys the Rights we have from* Magna Charta, *to*
D   *imprifon*

·n pri∫on tho∫e that are not Members of the.r Hou∫e,
·nan .t does, by confining tho∫e .l.at are, ∫ince the ∫ame
Cu∫tem ·h·at pleads for one may be alledg'd in defence
of t·c o·her, and the People who a e repre∫ented can-
·ot have Preten∫ions to greater Priviledges than tho∫e
·l.at repre∫ent 'em Either all Confinements order'd by
·ie Hou∫e, mu∫t be agreeable to Magna Charta, or
none can be, ∫ince the ∫ame Argument that de∫troys
One, di∫anulls All, and we mu∫t either allow the Judgment of Parliaments for a Tryal by our Peers, or
own no ∫uch Tryal has been made u∫e of in Parliamentary Proceedings that were previous to Commitments.

Whether they have invaded our Rights contrary to Magna Charta, and in ∫uch in∫tances as are a
Subver∫ion of our Con∫titution, will be evident to
us, if we look over the Catalogue of their Pri∫oners,
and examine the cau∫e of their Commitment The
five Kenti∫h Gentlemen, who∫e Ca∫e I am now
con∫idering, were impri∫on'd for a Fact no more
prohibited by the Laws of this Land, than praying for the King, or that God would direct the
Con∫ultations of the Parliament, to the advancement of the Safety, Honour, and Welfare of our
Sovereign and his Kingdoms It would be too te-
dious to de∫cend to particulars, of the great number which might here be taken notice of, as pertinent to my purpo∫e, I ∫hall mention only two,
Mr Pa∫c: -l nd Mr Har t ice The former wa
∫ent to the Tower, and kept there to the end of the
Se∫∫ions, for not giving in his Accounts after the
manner pre∫crib'd by the Commi∫∫ioners of Accounts, pur∫uant to an Act of Parliament The
latter was committed, and continued likewi∫e in
his Confinement till the end of the Se∫∫ion, for being faulty (as the Hou∫e of Commons thought) in
the di∫charge of his Office, in an in∫tance of taking
Bail. After his Confinement, his Accounts which
he

he had p ſſed were examined, and they were made another Charge againſt him. Whether thoſe Gentlemen were faulty or no, it concerns not me here to enquire Mr *Paſchal* has printed his Caſe, and 'tis a very hard one, the Crime for which he was ſent to the *Tower* was for not doing what was not in his power to do. But tho' he and others were guilty, 'tis certain that the puniſhing of them after that manner is neverthelefs an Injury to the Publick If Mr *Paſchal* was guilty of Contempt, and puniſhed thus for not obeying an Act made in the Seſlion of another Parliament, and Mr *Whita-cre* for being faulty in the diſcharge of his Office, may they not for the ſame reaſon charge all with Contempt who diſobey Acts of Parliament, or are faulty in the execution of their Offices, and puniſh them after the ſame manner ? Either they claim ſuch a Power as this, or they do not If they do not claim ſuch a Power, as the Right of the Commons of *England*, then they own that they have been injurious to thoſe Gentlemen in impri-ſoning them, and deſtroying that great and funda-mental Right which they have to the Liberty of their Perſons If they do claim ſuch a Power, they may ſeem to aſſume a Power which overthrows our whole Conſtitution This will be manifeſt, when we conſider the ſeveral Inſtances wherein ɩt ſubverts the Laws, the Rights and Liberties of the People

Anſw *The Liſt of the Priſoners committed to Parliament might be ten times as great, and yet the Priſoners under the ſame Gult, and the Gentlemen that had 'em taken into Cuſtody juſtified in their Pro-ceedings, ſince the ſame Authority that entitles 'em to confine one, may make it lawful for 'em to commit more But I cannot be induc'd by any means to believe the Kentiſh Petition was only a Prayer for the King and the Safety of the People, when it tended to make a difference between 'em, and preſcrib'd the giving Supplies,*

D ɩ

to their Confideration, who fate as Judges to confult when they were neceffa.y Particulars are things he carnot mak out, therefore he fpeaks in general, tho' at the fame time he flies from the particular Cafe of the Kentifh men to that of Mr. Whitacre and Mr Pafchal The firft is too well known, for the great Eftate he has lately acquir'd in a Poft of no very great Salary, and the laft is remarkable enough for Actions when Commiffroner of the Prize Offce, not to juftifie their Commirment Mr Pafchal, w.thout doubt, could have given in a fatisfactory Account in relation to the Prizes taken in the Streights, was not a certain Great Man who has rais'd his Fortunes by that gainful Expedition, at the bottom of the Plot, and Mr Whitacre could have done the Nation very fignal Service in relation to Capt in Kidd's Affairs, had he taken better Security for the Appearance of a Prifoner, that would have let us into the knowledge of fome Great Mens Practices that were Accomp'ices with him But they knew their bufinefs, One was Rich, and would not detect thofe that had made him fo, and t'other was Poor, and would not impeach him that was in a capacity of making him Rich. To what end therefore has the Parliament a Power to give Money for the Service of the Nation, if they have not likewife a Power to call thofe Perfons to an Account, that either mifapply it themfelves, or permit corrupt ufes of it in others?

Firft, It may be thought an Incroachment on the Power Legiflative For where the Commons are pleafed to inflict fuch a Punifhment for the violation of a Statute, as is not mentioned in the Statute, and was never defigned by the Legiflators, there they may feem to affume an Authority at leaft equal to that of the Legiflative To create a new Punifhment, and fuperadd it to a Law, may be allowed to be the Act of a Power equal to that which made it, and in the prefent Cafe fome may reckon it in fome fenfe greater, fince that Addition

lition makes it a Law with a Punishment *ex post facto*, which is a Power inconsistent with the Freedom of a People, and therefore is never made use of by our Legislators

Answ. The Commons have one part, and that the most material, of the Legislative Power in their hands, they contrive Laws, and put 'em into Form, and might be said actually to make *em, were not the Concurrence of the Two other Estates of the Nation altogether necessary towards the Enacting them And how they can encroach upon their own Authority, is beyond my Sphere to determine, since we generally look upon Encroachments to be an Invasion of other Peoples Rights, and not our own.*

Secondly, It may be deem'd an Encroachment on the Power and Rights of the King He by our Constitution has the supreme and sole executive Power He is *Caput & Salus Reipublicæ*. The Laws are his, and the Execution of them, wherein the Safety and Freedom of his People consists, are committed to Him, and those who derive their Authority from him Where ever therefore any part of his People take upon them to inflict Punishments without being authorized by him, or, which is the very same thing by his Laws, some may think that his Rights are thereby invaded, and his Majesty leslened, not only by that Invasion, but likewise by his being thereby made, instead of a Ruler of a brave and free People, a Titular King of poor and contemptible Slaves

Answ. The King is by every Subject's acknowledgement the Supreme Head of his Kingdoms but the Commons Imprisonment of People who made too free with Gentlemen in their high Station, does not affect the Royal Supremacy, or take any thing from the respect that is due to it It's true indeed, they do not represent the King as the ordinary Magistrate, but they assist him, are his Counsellors, and, such a part of his very

Com-

Compofition, *that he cannot fubfift without 'em, and certainly may be allow'd the fame Privilege as every Officer of Juftice is permitted the ufe of*

Thirdly, Some may account this an Invafion of the Rights and Liberties of the Kingdom, and fuch a one perhaps as deftroys Freedom, and introduces downright Slavery It may be worth *Englifh*-mens while to confider, whether they can form to themfelves any other Notion of a State of *Freedom* and Slavery, than that in the former, Men are governed by Laws made by their *Reprefentatives*, and are liable to no Punifhments but what are prefcrib'd by the Laws of that State and in the latter, that they have no certain Rule to walk by, but are fubject to the meer Will of One or More who claim a Power and Dominion over them Ii they find thefe Notions to be true, they will do well to confider again, Whether they can avoid making this Inference, That they who affume a Power to punifh a People who live under the direction of the Laws, without a Rule or Law, deftroy the Rights and Liberties of the People, take away their Freedom, and reduce them to a perfect State of Slavery ?

Anfw *The Rights and Liberties of the Kingdom are inviolably preferv'd by 'em, unlefs keeping the Ballance even between Lords and Commons be an Invafion of 'em, and any perfon that has any Gratitude, in return for their Noble and Generous Refolutions this laft Seffions, will never make ufe of any expreffions to decry what I is got 'em fuch Immortal Praife in the chiefeft Courts of* Chriftendom *If a Man fhould threaten to fire my Houfe, it's my bufinefs to take him up by way of prevention, not to ftay till he has executed his defign, that the Law may have its immediate Courfe with him · I probably may be ruin'd whilft I intend to proceed regularly againft him, therefore it's neceffary fometimes to take out of the common Road, and fo*

*cure Maleconcents from doing any harm, by Commit-
ments, &c*

Againſt what I have here ſaid, 'tis, I know, generally objected, That Juſtices of the Peace, Judges, and others, are allow'd to impriſon Freemen,
without being impeach'd of deſtroying that Liberty which they enjoy by *Magna Charta*, and the
Common Law of this Land Why then theſe Out-
criesagainſt the *Honourable Houſe of Commons?* The
Anſwer is very plain and eaſie The former are
Officers appointed by the King, who is inveſted
with the whole executive Power, to preſerve the
Peace of the Kingdom , and the latter are com-
miſſioned to do the ſame, and to preſide in his
Courts, and to adminiſter Juſtice to his Subjects,
which 'tis impoſſible for them to do without having a Power given them to confine evil and re-
bellious Subjects The lower Houſe of Parliament
is no Court, has no need of ſuch Power, being
call'd by the King to aſſiſt him with their Counſel
in Affairs of the greateſt moment and weight, to
bear a part in the Legiſlature, and to repreſent the
Grievances of the Nation, and deſire to have them
redreſſed , but not to redreſs them themſelves, by
taking upon them to puniſh Offenders If Judges,
or Juſtices of the Peace, or others who are entruſted with this Power, exceed their Commiſſion,
and are oppreſſive and injurious to the Subject,
there is a ſuperiour Juriſdiction to appeal to for
ſatisfaction, and Laws to determine whether Injury has been done or no But if a Houſe of Commons will puniſh thus without Law, there is no
Authority or Power on Earth from which Relief
may be had by Appeal, which in our Conſtitution
is a very good reaſon againſt their having ſuch a
Power , for the Lord-Chief-Juſtice *Huſſey* tells us,
That Sir *John Markham* told King *Edward* IV. that
he could not arreſt a Man, either for Treaſon or
Felony,

Felony, as a Subject might, becaufe that if the King did wrong, the Party could not have his Action againft him.

Anfw *If Juftices of Peace are cloath'd with the Power of Imprifoning without Procefs, &c. what fhould They be who fit at the Helm to infpect their Proceedings, and have it in their power to punifh 'em, by calling them to an Account for Abufes or Maleadminiftration? They are no Court of Judicature, but they are part of thofe Eftates from whence all Courts of Judicature belonging to this Nation have had their firft Eftablifhment, and ought to have the Preference, as much as the* thing created *is inferiour to* Him *that made it As for Sir* John Markham's *Obfervation, that the Subject can have no Action againft the King, the many Law-Suits we have feen commenc'd lately between the* King *and the* Subject *make appear to the contrary, for otherwife a Prince may do what he pleafes, and feize upon any one's Eftate without any manner of Right to it*

It may be farther urg'd, That as Judges having a Power to fettle and determine Property, is a reafon why they fhould have a Power to imprifon, becaufe the one is impracticable without the other. So the Houfe of Commons not having a Power to determine concerning Property, is a reafon why they fhould not have a Power to imprifon. *Cui non convenit minus, ei non majus convenit*, is a Maxim among the Logicians, and is a good Argument in the prefent Cafe. If the Houfe of Commons have no Power over our Goods, then *a fortiori* not over our Perfons to imprifon them, becaufe they are much more valuable than either Goods or Lands. This *Chrift* himfelf declares, when he tells us, that *the Body is more than Raiment*, where by *Raiment* the *Canonifts* underftand all outward things whatfoever Our Laws alfo make this clear, and give the preference to the *Body* 'Tis

a Rule in Law, that *Corporalis injuria non recipit
æstimationem e futuro* So as if the Question be not
for a Wrong to the Person, the Law will not com-
pel him to sustain it, and afterwards accept Remedy, for the Law holds no Damage a sufficient
Recompence for a Wrong that is Corporal There
are Cases in Law that prove this Rule if one menace me in my Goods, or that he will burn the
Evidence of my Land which he hath in his Custo-
dy, unless I will make unto him a Bond, there I
cannot avoid the Bond by pleading of this Menace
But if he restrains my Person, or threatens me with
Battery, or with burning my House which is a
Protection for my Person, or with burning an In-
strument of Manumission, which is an Evidence
of my Enfranchisement, upon these Menaces I
shall avoid the Bond by Plea So if a Trespasser
drive my Beast over another Man's Ground, and
I pursue to rescue it there, I am a Trespasser to
him on whose Ground I am But if a Man assault
my Person, and I for my Safety fly over into no-
ther Man's Ground, there I am no Trespasser to
him for *quod quis in tuitione sui corporis fecerit, jure
id fecisse existimatur*, What a Man do in defence of his Person, he is reckon'd to do it
fully Nay, which is more, the Common Law
did favour the Liberty, not only of Freemen but
even of the Persons of Bondmen and Villains who
have no Right of Property in Lands or Goods, as
Freemen have The Lord by the Law could not
maim his Villain, nay, if he commanded another
to beat him, and he did it, the Villain should
have his Action of Battery for it against him if
the Lord made a Lease for Years to his Villain, if
he pleaded with him, if he tender'd him to be a
Champion for him in a Writ of Right, any of
these Acts, and many others, were in the Law En-
franchisements, and made those Villains Freemen
From all which it appears, That the Law has a
E   greater

greater regard to our Perfons than Eftates, which, as I faid, is a good Argument why the Houfe of Commous. who have nothing to do in regulating or determining our other Properties, fhould not have a Power over the Liberty of our Perfons

Anſw Tˡe Commons have a Rightˡ to determine and fettle Properties, if the many Bills paſs'd in their Houſe relating to Entails of Eſtates, and the many Plead-ings by the Learned in tˡe Law befˡore 'em as Judges, can entitle 'em to it Tˡey cannot indeed alter a Set-tlement without Application made to 'em by tˡe Par-ties concernˡd, neitˡer can a Judge give his definitive Sentence in a Cauſe, witl out it be brought into Court As they are authˡorizˡd to be Judges in matteɩs of Eſtate that are doubˡful, ſo it is appɩˡent from Exɩmple, and one of a freſher Date, the Caſe of Sir John Fenwick, tˡˡy can go beyoˡd Impriſonment of tˡe Body, and puniſb it witⁱ Death If theɩefoɩe thˡy can Attaint wheɩe tˡe Laws tl at have been made are of no foɩce, and the Interpret:.ion of 'em is in favour of the Crⁱ-minal, tˡey may ceɩtainly Impriſon by his own ap-provˡd Maxim, ſⁱˡcc Confinement is a buſineſs of leˡ's Conceɩn than that wl ⁱch is incompaɩablj ſuperioɩ to it, (viz) Iɩflⁱcᵗⁱon of Deᵗth

Sir John Foɩt fcue, the Learned Chancellor to King Heⁱ, VI writing (*de Dom Polⁱt & Regal*) of this Kingdom, ſaith, *Regnum illud in omnibus Natiⁱon m & Regum temporⁱtus, uˡ lem quⁱbus nunc r gⁱ.ur legⁱbus & confuˡˡuˡdⁱⁱbus regebatuⁱ* This Saying wⁱⁱl not ſure cur Tⁱmcs, we cⁱnnot ſay, 'Thⁱt the Laws and cⁱfⁱⁱms vⁱhⁱch we arc governˡd by, are the very ſamⁱ wⁱᵗh thoſe by which this Kingdom wⁱs governˡd ⁱn the Timⁱs of all the former Kingⁱ nd the ſeveral Natⁱons that came in hⁱther The Powⁱr ⁱfſum'd by the Houſe of Commⁱns in ⁱⁱecutⁱng Iɩws, and impriſoning Men, is a vⁱⁱy new thing, and makes our pⁱeſent Stⁱte very diffⁱrent from our antⁱent Conſtitution

The

lute Power, and compellthem to that which is a-
gainſt the Right of their Freedom. To be free
from ſuch Force is the only Security Men have of
their Preſervation, and Reaſon bids them to look
on thoſe as Enemies to their Preſervation, who
would take away that Freedom which is the Fence
to it, and ſo conclude that they have a Will and
Deſign to take away every thing elſe, ſince that
Freedom is the Foundation of all the reſt.

Anſwer,

*The way to defeat the progreſs of Arbitrary Power, is
certainly to reſtrain it, but how thoſe Members who
have effectualy ſuppreſs'd it in others, have ſtood up ſo
Zealouſly for the Liberties of the People, and have
been ſuch hearty ſticklers for the Rights of the Commons of* England, *againſt the preſumptive Encroachments of the* Lords, *can be ſaid to take the ſame impe-
tuous Meaſures, it is not in my Power to divine.
Neither is it my purpoſe, to diſpute the* Wiſdom and
Juſtice of *their Predeceſſors, tho' it is my Buſineſs
to vindicate the Proceedings of thoſe that are now in
Authority, yet if Supplies to the* King *without any Bur-
then to the Subject, a ready concurrence to Aſſiſt his Confederates, without coming into an open Rupture with
thoſe that were his their Enemies, and the ſincereſt Endeavours for the continuance of the Publick Peace, while
they are making proviſion for our Defence, be not as much
as has been done in any Parliament, nay, farther, in
any Age whatſoever, and preferable to any antecedent
Reſolutions, then Patriots that come after theſe worthy
Gentlemen, and ſucceed 'em in their care for the ſecurity of the Nations, muſt deſpair of doing any thing
that can be praiſe worthy ſince, if theſe are accounted
the Nations* Enimies, *it is not in the Power of Humanity to be its* Friend.

From what I have here delivered concerning
the Power of impriſoning in the Lower Houſe,
'tis evident, I think, that if Petitioning, as the *Kentiſh* Gentlemen did, had been an illegal Act, and
the

the Punifhment enjoin'd by the Law had been Imprifonment, yet it belong d not to them to inflict that Punifhment, but to make application (as they have always done heretofore) to have the Law executed gainft them But if what they did was ftrictly agreeable to Law, this will make their Commitment a greater Violation of the Rights of the Community. That it was fo, will appear, when we confider

Anfwer,

He has hitherto been deliver'd *like the Mountain in the Fable, noting but infignificancies and Productions of ridiculous Conf quences, and affirms he has made out the matter ne took in Hind to a Tittle, when the Reader has reafon to have other Sentiments, and entertain Notions of another Proportion than what he lays down for undoubted Truths Thofe that can Command others to profecute as Attorny Generals, &c have an indifputable Title to Imprifon, fince Profecution is precedent to Punifhment, and confequently is of more moment than Imprifonment, which only a bare Confinement of the Perfon without affecting his Life, or Eftate, which are in Danger from it, and the Old Maxim holds good, that* omne Majus continet in fe Minus

The Second thing propos'd, *the Subject's Right of Petitioning.* This Right I take to be as large and ample a one, and what will as little bear controverting, as any thing that we can think of, fince 'tis juftified by the Law of Nature, the Practice of all States in the World, and is allowed by the Laws of this Land

'Tis certain that nothing can be more agreeable to Nature, and a plainer Dictate of Reafon, than that thofe who apprehend themfelves aggriev'd be allow'd a liberty to approach thofe by Petition who know their Grievances, or perhaps are the Authors of them, and confequently able to redrefs them. When Men enter'd firft into Society, and

gave

gave up that Right which they had to secure themselves in the State of Nature, 'tis manifest that they
did it for the preservation of Property, which is
the end of Government This necessarily suppo-
ses and indeed requires that People should have
Property, without which they must be suppos'd
to lose that by entering into Society which was
the end for which they enter'd into it If Men
enter'd into Society to preserve it, and there are
are so entitled to it, that (as a very Learned and
Ingenious Author tells us) *The supreme Power
cannot take from any Man any part of his Property
without his own consent* , Can any Absurdity be so
gross, as to imagin, that Men gave up their Right
to pray for Redress, if they thought themselves injur'd intheir Properties ? Or that thesupreme Power may hinder them to pray for that which they
have not a right to deprive them of ? Wherever
therefore any Government is establifhed there
the natural Right which People had to secure
what was their own, must be so far at least continued, as to allow them a liberty to Petition for
what they think their Right, because this is a Pri-
viledge which they could not give up, when they
enter'd into Society And where there has been
no government but the Prince's Will, even there
this Right has seemed so natural and agreeable to
Reason, that it has not been denied. This might
be seen in all the Arbitrary Governments of the
World. In the *Roman* Empire *Julius Cesar*, when
he was in the heighth of his Power,and made himfelf *Perpetual Dictator*, permitted the People to represent the Hardships that were put upon them,
and pray for redress And in the Reign of other
Princes who exercis'd a Despotick Power, whilst
the *Lex Regia* prevail'd *refcribere Principi*, to petition the Prince, and set forth their Grievances,
was allowed their Subjects as the natural Right
of Mankind.

F   Anf.

Anſw No Man living contraverts *the Subjects right of* Petitioning, *but that is not the Caſe in hand, it's the Writers buſineſs to prove that* Libelling *is Lawful* The moſt virulent Piece of Treaſon imaginable may go under the Name of a Petition, and be gloſs'd over with a Specious fair Title, when the contents of it are embitter'd againſt thoſe in Authority, and aim at the very Foundation of the Regal Supremacy In Charles the Martyr's time Faction skulk'd abroad under the Covert of Remonſtrances, and Petitions to Kings were as full of Blaſphemies, as thoſe which were ſent up from the Pulpits to the divine Majeſty, the Removal of evil Councillors was the pretence they made uſe of when the downfal of Monarchy was what was rea'ly intended, as what the Kentiſh Gentlemen deſign'd by finding fault with the proceedings of Parliament and making uſe of the Voice of the People, to put down Sr Stephens Chappel over their Repreſentatives Head, looks very much like Something of the ſame complexion As for Julius Cæſar in his Perpetual Dictatorſhip he permitted the People to have Acceſs to him on Account of real Grievances, but when one Popilius whiſper'd unſeaſonable Advice in his Ear, he ordered him immediately to be puniſh'd by the Lictor, as an interfering Coxcomb, and one who concern'd himſelf with buſineſs above his Sphere Marcus Antonius likewiſe cauſd Cicero to be Aſſaſſinated, and put to Death, tho' he had been Conſul of Rome, which is a Poſt of Honour ſomething above a Kentiſh Juſtice of the Peace, becauſe he did ſpargere voces in Vulgus, inſinuate to the People, that Anthony's Proceedings were Irregular, that it tended to ſubvert the Conſtitution of the Roman Republick, &c.

If this Right be natural, the People of *England*, who have loſt as little by entring into Society as any others, muſt have as juſt and ample a Claim to it as any Nation in the World. That they have

a

i Right to reprefent their Sufferings, and pray for
a Relaxation of them, is evident from the Opini-
ons of our Sages of the Law, from what our Kings
have permitted and declared, and what has been
declared and enacted in Parliament

Our Books are very clear in this matter. My
Lord Chief-Juſtice *Hobbart* tells us, That 'tis lawful for any Subject to petition the King for redreſs
in an humble manner , for (ſays he) *Acreſs to the
Sovereign muſt not be ſhut up in caſe of the Subject's
diſtreſs.* This Right was fully prov'd by the Learned Councel at the Trial of the ſeven Biſhops,
and allow'd by the Judges It was one of the
Crimes for which the *Spencers* were baniſhed, that
they hinder'd the King from receiving and anſwer-
ing Petitions from Great Men and others , and
one Article againſt the Lord *Strafford* was, That
he iſſued out a Proclamation and Warrant of re-
ſtraint to inhibit the Kings Subjects to come to the
Fountain their Sovereign, to deliver their Complaints of Wrongs and Oppreſſions

*Anſw. The Right of Petitioning for Aſſiſtance in Caſes
of imminent Danger, is not only agreeable to the Law
of Nature, but directly commanded by the great Law
of Self-preſervation But to diſperſe Fears and jea-
louſies when there is no occaſion, to call out for Help,
like the Shepherd's Boy in the Fable, when there are no
Wolves at hand, is to divert our Protectors from aſſiſting us when there are imminent Dangers that
actually threaten us. In the BISHOPS Caſe,
thoſe Right Reverend Fathers of the Church ſtood ac-
cus'd on account of their indiſpenſable Duty They petition'd the King as the Directors of his Conſcience,
and his ſpiritual Adviſers, in relation to His Majeſty's
Declaration, but did not interfere with his Prerogative, as the Wiſe Men of Kent did with that of
their Repreſentatives, and it is but too viſible what
ſide their Advocate inclines to, when he produces an
Article that was brought againſt the Lord Strafford,*

who

*who was guiltlefs of the Offences laid to his Charge, tho'
he was murder'd for 'em, to juftifie the Right of Libelling Governments, and bantering the Proceedings of
Parliaments*

As the Sages of the Law have told us That 'tis
our undoubted Right, fo have our Kings in all
Ages permitted us by Petition to inform them of
our Grievances In the Reigns of King *Edw* II
and King *Edw* III fuch Petitions were frequent,
and then even *Ireland* was allow'd to reprefent
their Grievances, and petition for a Parliament

Doctor *Burnet*, the Learned Bishop of *Salisbury*
informs us That King *Henry* VIII told his Sub
jects, when in Arms againft him in *York fhire*, that
they ought not to have rebell'd, but to have ap-
lied themfelves to him by Petition

King *James* I by a Proclamation publifh'd the
11th year of his Reign, begins thus *The Complaints lately exhibited to Us by certain Noblemen and
others of Our Kingdom of* Ireland, *fuggefting Difor-
ders and Abufes, as well in the Proceedings of the late-
begun Parliament, as in the Martial and Civil Go
vernment of the Kingdom, We did receive with all
extraordinary Grace and Favour* And by another
Proclamation he declares , That *'twas the Right of
his Subjects to make their immediate Addreffes to him
by Petition* And in another he tells his People,
That *his own, and the Ears of his Privy Council, did
ftill continue open to the juft Complaints of his People
- ------And that they were not confin'd to Times and
Meetings in Parliament, nor reftrain'd to particular
Grievances.*

It appears by the Lords Journals in the Year
1640 that the Houfe of Lords both Spiritual and
Temporal, *Nemine Contradicente*, voted Thanks
to thofe Lords who petitioned the King at *York* to
call a Parliament And that King by his Declaration 1644 declared his Royal Will and Plea-
fure,

fure, That all his loving Subjects, who have any
juft Caufe to prefent, or complain of any Grievances or Oppreſſions may freely addreſs themſelves by their humble Petition to his moſt Sacred
Majeſty, who will gracioufly hear their Complaints

On *Wedneſday* the 27th of *October*, 1680 it was
refolv'd in the Houfe of Commons, *Nemine Contradicente, That it is, and EVER hath been, the undoubted Right of the Subjects of* England *to petition
the King for the calling and fitting of Parliaments and
redreſſing of Grievances* 'Twas then likewiſe reſolv'd,
*Nemine Contradicente That to traduce fuch Petition-
ing as a violation of Duty, and to reprefent it to his
Majefty as tumultuous and feditious, is to betray the
Liberty of the Subject, and contribute to the Defign of
fubverting the antient legal Conftitution of this Kingdom, and introducing Arbitrary Power* On the *Fri-
day* following (as we find in the fame Journal) it
appearing to the Houfe, upon the examination of
feveral Witneffes at the Bar thereof, upon the Evidence againſt Sir *Francis Withins*, as well as upon
his own Confeſſion, that he had prefented an Addrefs to his Majeſty expreſſing an Abhorrency to
petition his Majeſty for the calling and fitting of
Parliaments, 'twas refolv'd, *That Sir* Francis Withins, *by promoting and prefenting to his Majefty an
Addrefs expreſſing his ſa. 1 Abhorrency, hath betrayed
the undoubted Rights of the Subjects of* England.
'Twas moreover order'd, that he fhould be expell'd the Houfe, and that he fhould receive his
sentence upon his knees

Anfw. *I have too great a deference for the Sages of
the Law, not to agree with them that 'tis part of the
Priviteges that a Subject enjoys, to petition his Prince
but muft take the freedom of thinking that in* Edward
*the 2d, and 3d's days they had not the liberty of fo fre-
quently making Addreſſes to the Throne, had there been
any* Colepeppers *or* Pollhills, &c *to take the bufi-*
neſ.

nefs of Privy-Councellors upon 'em, without a Privy-Councellor's Understanding. And tho' what the Bifhop of Salisbury *writes may carry an Authority with it in relation to King* Henry *the* 8th's *Speech to his Subjects, that Prelate can remember a Perfon he is very well acquainted with, did not take the Advice, but appear'd in open Arms againft his Sovereign.* King James *the* 1ft's *two Proclamations have likewife no more in* 'em *to make for his purpofe, than what has preceded, fince they were grounded upon* Juft *Complaints, which are exclufive of the* Kentifh *Petitioners, who had no Grounds or Reafons for their Arrogance, and the Quotation from the Lords* Journals, *if we confider the Times the Refolution was made in,* (viz.) *the very Infancy of Rebellion, and beginning of the Civil War which was then in projection* The Refolutions *of the Year* 1680 *are much of the fame ftamp, if we confider from what hands they came, and thofe Member that could juftifie the Treafons and Seditious Speeches of* Stephen Colledge, *are not to be fuppos'd to be Enemies to Remonftrances againft the Proceedings of Supreme Authority, when their very Being tends to Confufion and Anarchy.*

This Right of the Subject to petition, is farther confirm'd by the Statute-Law of this Land, particularly in an Act made in the 13th year of King *Charles* II. the Enacting part of which I will here at large fet down, becaufe 'tis a plain Declaration of the Subjects Right in the Cafe of the Petition now under our Confideration.

'Be it Enacted, &c That no perfon or perfons
'whatfoever fhall from and after the firft of *Auguft*
'1661. folicit, labour, or procure the getting of
'Hands, or other Confent, of any Perfons above
'the number of Twenty or more, to any Petition,
'Complaint, Remonftrance, Declaration, or other
'Addrefs to the King, or both or either Houfes of
'Parliament, FOR ALTERATION OF MATTERS
'ESTA

' ESTABLISHED BY LAW IN CHURCH OR
' STATE, unlefs the Matter thereof have firft been
' confented to, and order'd by three or more Jufti-
' ces of the County, or by the major part of the
' Grand-Jury of the County or Divifion of the
' County where the fame fhall arife, at their pub-
' lick Affizes, or General Quarter Seffions , or if
' arifing in London, by the Lord Mayor, Aldermen,
' or Commons in Common-Council affembled ;
' and that no Perfon or Perfons whatfoever fhall
' repair to his Majefty, or both or either Houfes
' of Parliament, upon pretence of prefenting or
' delivering any Petition, Complaint, Remon-
' ftrance, or Declaration, or other Addreffes, ac-
' companied with exceffive Numbers of People,
' not at any one time above the number of ten Per-
' fons upon pain of incurringa Penalty not excee-
' ding the Sum of one hundred Pounds in Money,
' and three Months Imprifonment.

' Provided always, That this Act, or any thing
' therein contain'd, fhall not be conftru'd to ex-
' tend to debar or hinder any Perfon or Perfons,
' not exceeding the number of Ten aforefaid, to
' prefent ANY PUBLICK OR PRIVATE GRIE-
' VANCE OR COMPLAINT TO ANY MEMBER
' OR MEMBERS OF PARLIAMENT, after his
' Election, and during the Continuance of the
' Parliament, or to the King's Majefty, for any
' Remedy to be thereunto had. ---

Anfw *The Act in the 13th Year of King* Charles
the 2d was exprefly defign'd againft tumultuous Peti-
tioning , as may be feen from the Preamble, which
lets us into the Intentions of it , and becaufe it was
not to be fuppos'd that Juftices of Peace would fet their
hands to every ridiculous Whimfey fome Malecontents
might entertain in relation to Governments, was word-
ed after that manner   But the County of Kent *has*
furnifh'd us with Examples to the contrary, and made
appear that there are more than twenty Juftices that

are

*are Fools enough in it to subscribe what is against its
Profit, and are ready to run mad for a new War, when
the Charges of the last have been enough to make 'em
sober.*

Concerning this Statute we may observe Four
things First, That it allows (as Mr Serjeant *Levins* observ'd in the Trial of the seven Bishops,
and we are taught by several other good Authorities) th t by the Law of the Land before, it was
th sertl'd and undoubted Right of the Subjects of
E and to apply themselves to the King, or either or both Houses of Parliament, by Petition, to
have their Grievances redress'd Secondly, That
where it limits this Power of the Subject, and requires that the Petition shall be consented to and
order'd by three or more Justices of the County, or
by the major part of the Grand-Jury of the County,
or Division of the County where the same Matter
shall arise, or by the Lord Mayor, Aldermen, or
Commons in Common-Council assembled, if it a-
rise in *London* 'tis only in a particular Case, where
the Address is for *Alteration of Matters establish'd by
Law in Church or State.* Thirdly, That even in
this Case the Concurrence of those Persons is not
requir'd, unless it be where there are more than
Twenty r ands to the Petition. Fourthly,
That the Act extends not to Grievances or Complaints either Publick or Private, but that they
may be presented to the King or Parliament, without any of those previous Formalities, provided
that the Petition or Address be not presented by
more than Ten.

Answ. Mr *Serjeant* Levins *his Observatins at the
Trial of the Seven Bishops are taken notice of very
mal a propos in reference to the Five* Kentish *men,
because their Case is as different from each other, as a
Libel to create Tumults, is from an Address to beseech*

H t

His Majesty not to impose upon one's Conscience, and tho' the Petition (*as they call it*) *was lawful in the Manner or* Form *of presenting i' b.. 'g not brought up by more than* Ten *, et it was Illeg t tl e D-fgn, as well as exceptionable from some words woub were reflective on the Honour of Parliaments in it.*

Having mention'd this Act, which (tho' made to limit and reftrain the Subject, and curtail his natural Right of petition) is a full Declar.. . of the Peoples Right to apply themfelves to the King or Parliament *by Petition, for the Redrefs or their Grievances, and for obtaining fuch things as they apprehend neceffary or beneficial to the Safety or Well being of the Nation* I need not urge any other Authorities, nor take notice even of that Act pafs'd fince the Revolution, wherein the Rights of the People are contain'd, and that of Petitioning is declar'd to be one 'Tis evident to any Reader of the moft ordinary Capacity, that the *Kentifh* Petition is warranted by the Law of the Land, and fo plainly within the Letter of that Act, that thofe Men are forc'd to acknowledge it, who take a great deal of pains to juftifie all the Proceedings of the Houfe of Commons Was it not then (to ufe the Words of *Legion*) *illegal, and a notorious Breach of the Liberty of the Subject, and fetting up a Difpenfing Power in the* Houfe of Commons, *to imprifon Men who were not their Members, by no Proceedings but a Vote of the Houfe, and to continue them in Cuftody* SINE DIE? A late Pamphleteer, by way of Anfwer to this, tells us, That *to fay this is done by a fingle Vote without other Proceedings, is meer Babling and Nonfenfe, for Imprifonment is the firft ftep in order to future Proceedings, and practi'd by every fingle Magiftrate.* What does this Scribler mean? Were not thofe Petitioners imprifoned by a Vote of the Houfe, without any other Proceedings? Was there any Indictment, or legal

G Pro-

Procefs to try whether they were guilty of any
Trefpafs againft the Law ? For what reafon does
he tell us, that *Imprifonment is the firft ftep in order
to future Punifhment* ? Would he thereby infinuate
that their Crime was fuch as might be further
punifh'd by Law ? Their Judges in St *Stephen's*
Chappel knew very well that it could not If it
could, why were they not proceeded againft ?
Why were they kept in Prifon till the end of the
Seffion ? If they could not, why fhould they be
imprifon'd at all, fince it could be in order to no
future Proceedings ? But he tells us, That *this is
pra&is'd by every Magiftrate* 'Tis true, they imprifon, but 'tis to keep the Peace, and in order to
future Punifhment , and what they do, is allowed
and warranted by the Law of the Land From
what I have already faid in this Difcourfe, 'twill
appear how abfurd it would be to make this an
Argument for the Commons having fuch a Power
as they have us'd in imprifoningthofe Gentlemen
The Reader will from hence judge whether *Legion* or this Author is moft guilty of *Babling* and
Nonfenfe The Defign of this Pamphleteer is to
throw all the Dirt he can on the late Miniftry, to
bring them under the Odium of the Nation, (a
Work which the *Jacobites*, the *French Party*, and
Papifts of *England* are now, and have been a great
while very intent upon) and to recommend the
Proceedings of the Houfe of Commons, and the
prefent Miniftry to the People. Thefe are the
Perfons pointed at in the Title of his Book, which
he calls, *England's Enemies Expos'd, and its true
Friends and Patriots Defended* If he fhew no better Judgment in difcovering who deferve to be
called the *Enemies*, who the *Friends* of *England*,
than in laying the Charge of *Babbling* and *Nonfenfe*. he will do as little Service to *England* in
helping her to make any ufeful Difcovery of her
real Friends and Enemies, as he has done to his
Friends

Friends by his poor , his paltry, and palpable
Flatteries   The Prince of Darknefs, when he
goes up and down to do Mifchief, and deftroy
the Kingdoms of the Earth, as he turns himfelf into
an Angel of Light, fo has he Enemies, *qui nigra
in candida vertunt*, little Hirelings, whofe Task it
is to call *Evil Good, and Good Evil* ; to deceive
with falfe Colours that he may be the better a-
ble to deftroy   To give People a little tafte of
this Panegyrift's Impofitions, and the Judgment
he has made of Men, I will only take notice here
that he commends the *Fair Character* of Mr *J--n
H-w*, and calls him (who moft certainly call'd the
Treaty made by the King *a Felonious Confpiracy)
A Zealous Patriot*, and one *who will not exceed his
Duty* , that he reprefents the Spe--er as a Perfon
deferving *the honourable Character of an honeft*
Englifh *Gentleman, a Champion for Liberty, and a
true Patriot, without Difguife, Collufion, or Self Intereft* , that *they whofe long Experience in Publick
Affairs gave them knowledge of the Methods employ'd
by* France *in former Reigns, to enflave* Europe, *are
beft able to prevent his Defigns in this* , that *tear-
ing up our Conftitution by the Roots* is the Work of
the late Miniftry , that they *have betray'd the
King*, and *carry on Purpofes deftructive to the Nation* , that if we have a *Porto Carero* in the Nation, 'tis He *who has done his utmoft to deliver us up
to* France, *by invefting the Moft Chriftian King with
a Power to feize us* , that 'tis He (meaning *L--d
Hall- ax*) to whom *French* Gold is given Strange
Effrontery ' Had Sir *Bar----w Sh--er* fpoken this,
I fhould not wonder at it , he, we know, when
the Lords were voted Guilty of High Crimes and
Mifdemeanours for the Treaty of Partition, and
an Impeachment was ordered, did not blufh to
fay openly in the Houfe, That the News of it
would be very unwelcom at *Verfailles.*

Anſw. *As for his Reflections on the* Pamphleteer *that anſwer'd* The preſent Diſpoſition of *Englanc* conſider'd, &c. *they are foreign to the purpoſe, and would almoſt perſuade one that it came from the ſame Hand. Had not I ſome knowledge of the Author, who is ſo far from being a* Jacobite, Papiſt, *or of the* French Party, *that he is hated by 'em, as a Perſon that has been all along employed by the Creatures of* this Government, *to make Diſcoveries of their Proceedings, and prevent their Deſigns To my knowledge his Pamphlet owes its birth to his Circumſtances , and had the* Court *made better Proviſion for him , he would ſcarce have fallen out with the* Courtier, *ana the* Lord Hallifax *would have had as good a Character from him, as Mr.* How *and the* Speaker, *had but his Perſion continu'd to come trowling in from the* Treaſury, *and he not found himſelf under a neceſſity of taking other Meaſures The Author of* Legion *and He probably might come from the ſame place of Inſtruction , ſince their Language is equally foul and ungentleman-like: But for the Reflection on Sir* Bartholomew Shower, *by ſuch a mean Compariſon, the Author of this very Pamphlet ſhews that he knows how to join in Conſort with the two Scribes before mention'd, who blended together would make an admirable ſort of a* Triumvirate.

But to return from this Digreſſion to the matter in hand. Thoſe who cannot deny that the Subject has a Right to Petition, yet juſtifie the Proceedings againſt thoſe who deliver'd the Petition, becauſe of its reproaching the honourable Houſe, and preſcribing Rules to our Legiſlators. The Reſolution of the Houſe of Commons concerning it was, that *'twas ſcandalous, inſolent, and ſeditious, tending to deſtroy the Conſtitution of Parliament, and to ſubvert the Eſtabliſhed Government of this Realm.* Before I come to a particular Examination

nation of this Refolution, I muſt crave leave to
make this Remark upon it, That this very Cen-
ſure, and the ſevere Treatment of the Petitioners,
ſhew us plainly into what hands we are fallen
We remember very well when it was, that Sir
Edward Seymour, then a Privy-Councellor, and
ſome others now in Power, learned the Trick of
giving hard Names to Petitions. What I here
hint at, I will endeavour to repreſent in the
ſhorteſt View I can, becauſe the matter will be
pertinent to the Subject I am treating of and will
give true *Engliſh*-men an opportunity of making
ſome Reflections which will be uſeful to us in the
preſent Circumſtances of our Affairs ' We cannot forget what great Concern the Commons of
England above Twenty Years ſince ſhewed for
the Proteſtant Religion, that their Zeal to preſerve it was ſeen in Four Parliaments, which
were diſſolv'd in a little more than the ſpace of
Two Years, by reaſon of their Warmth in proſecuting Popiſh Conſpiratois, and Labouring to ex-
clude the Duke of *York*, whoſe Succeſſion to the
Crown rais'd the hopes of Papiſts, and gave birth
to all their Plots.

Anſwer

*A Digreſſion indeed ' and which I am glad to ſee
him own, after having ſpent his Venom to no purpoſe
The* Reſolution *of the* Houſe of Commons *was Honourable, and it ſhews pla nly that we are fallen into
ſuch Hands as we may rely upon for Defence, without
the Aſſiſtance of ſuch intermeddlers* Si Edward
Seymour *keeps up to his* Old Loyal Principles, *ana
tho' he does not officiate as Privy Councellor to His
preſent Majeſty, is zealous for the Good of the Nation
as a Senator, and continues firm to his* Old Principles *of having an* Abhorrence *for Mutinous Aſ-
ſemblies, and Deſigns againſt the Government. which
ſuch reſtleſs Malecontents as our Author (who ſo zea-*
louſly

o

*louſly ſtands up in Vindication of Injuſtice in the Bill
of Excluſion againſt His late Majeſty when Duke of
York, and Preſumptive Heir of the Crown) are per-
petu.. .y contriving.*

The firſt was the long Parliament, which con-
ſiſted of Members ſo devoted to the Crown, that
they would have gratified it in any Demand whatſoever, had not the Meaſures taken to deſtroy *Holland*, the great Friendſhip contracted with *France*
by Mediation of the Duke of *York* , and the
Growth of Popery ſour'd their Tempers, and
given their Inclinations quite another Biaſs   After their Prorogation on the 28*th* of *December*,
1678 which was ſoon followed by a *Diſſolution*,
the next Parliament which begun at *Weſtminſter*
on the 6*th* of *March*, 1673 purſu'd the ſame Meaſures to ſecure the Religion and Laws of *England*,
and were for that reaſon prorogu'd on the 26*th*
of *May* following.

The People of *England* alarum'd at this, and
growing into greater Fears of the Conſpiracy
which the Parliament endeavour'd to prevent,
ſent Petitions to the King from ſeveral Places,
wherein they repreſented the Grievances of the
Nation, and pray'd for the ſitting of the Parliament to redreſs them   I ſhall take notice of the
Stile of one for all, *viz* That of the City of *London*, wherein they ſet forth that there is *a moſt
damnable and heliſh Popiſh* P L O T, *BRANCH'D
FORTH INTO THE MOST HORRID VIL-
LANIES, againſt his Majeſty's moſt Sacred Perſon, the* Proteſtant *Religion, and the well eſtabliſh'd
Government of his Realm, for which ſeveral of the
principal Conſpirate s ſtand impeach'd by Parliament
Therefore in ſuch a time when his Majeſty's Royal
Perſon, as alſo the* Proteſtant *Religion, and the Government of the Nation are in moſt eminent Danger,
they moſt humbly and earneſtly pray that the Parliamen*

o

ment which *is proroagu'd until* the 26th *Day of* January *may then fit, to try the Offenders, and to re-,refs all the most important Grievances, no otherwise to be redrefs'd* This Petition, which was a Roll of above 100 Yards in length, was prefented by Sir *Gilbert Gerrard,* and eight other Gentlemen of good note They all fail'd of the defir'd effect, for the Parliament was diffolv'd, and none other late till *October* following.

Anfwer.

How could the Members of the Long Parliament *be faid to be* devoted to the Crown, *when they were for altering the Succeffion, and ftriking at the very Foundation of* Monarchy *it felf, under the fpecious pretence of* Securing the Proteftant Religion ? *As for the* City of London's Petition, *thofe who remember their Practices at that time, can account for the Effects of it , and thofe who have any knowledge of their Proceedings even at this time, and how they had like to have been guilty of the fame Premunire with the* Kentifh *men, but for one fingle Common-Coun-cil-Man's Vote, cannot but be fatisfied they are as ripe for* Mutiny, *as they were for* Rebellion *at* Edge-hill-*Fight.*

The Men now in Power have not, it feems, forgotten how they refented thofe Petitions at that time. Their Meafures then are the very Precedents they copy after now Tho' 'twas then the Subject's Right to petition, as I have fhewn it is now , tno' the Petitioners took care to keep within the Bounds of the Law, yet a Proclamation iffu'd out on the 12th of *December,* 1679. to prohibit fuch *illegal and tumultuous Petitioning, as tending to Sedition and Rebellion.* Befides, care was taken to prevail upon their Friends to procure *Counter-Addreffes,* wherein the Subfcribers expreft their *Abhorrence of Petitioning*

Anfw

Anſwer

The Men then in Power preſeiv'd King Charles *the Second's Prerogitive, by oppoſing ſuch unjuſtifiable Proceedings, and thoſe in Authority now are ready to do the ſame by King* William'*s and if they take the ſame Meaſuics, they do but follow a good Copy, which render'd then* Predeceſſors *Fame of a Loyal Savour, and will deduce* their own *to Poſterity, without any other Aſſiſtance than its own Merit for it Conveyance.*

Theſe Meaſures that were taken to run down this Right of the Subject, and to ſubvert the Conſtitution of Parliament, together with the Diſpleaſure conceiv'd againſt ſome Men of great Poſts in the Law, and Figure in the Civil State, for acting Illegally, and giving *pernicious Councel* (as the Commons were pleas'd to term it) *to his Majeſty,* occaſion'd very warm Votes and Reſolutions in the next Parliament, which, after many Proroguations, ſate on the 21ſt of *October.* 1680 and continued ſitting to the 10th day of *January following*

Within ſix days after their Meeting. (*viz October* the 27th) immediately after they had agreed upon an Addreſs to his Majeſty, wherein they ex preſs'd their *Reſolution to purſue with a ſtrict and im partial Enquiry the execrable Popiſh Plot,* they pro ceeded to Votes about Petitions Then, as I ob- ſerv'd before, 'twas

" Reſolv'd, *Nemine Contradicente,* That it is, " and ever hath been, the undoubted Right of " the Subjects of *England,* to petition the King " for the calling and ſitting of Parliaments, and " redreſſing Grievances

" Reſolv'd,

" *Refolv'd*, That to traduce fuch Petitioning as
" a Violation of Duty, and to reprefent it to his
" Majefty as Tumultuous and Seditious, is to be-
" tray the Liberty of the Subject, and contributes
" to the Defign of fubverting the antient legal
" Conftitutions of this Kingdom, and introducing
" ARBITRARY POWER.

"*Order'd*, That a Committee be appointed to en-
" quire of all fuch Perfons as have offended againft
' thefe Rights of the Subjects.

The next day (*October* the 28th) Sir *Francis
Wythens*, as I have oblerv'd before, being found
Guilty in this particular, they voted him a *Betrayer of the Undoubted Rights of the Subjects of* England, and order'd him to be expell'd the Houfe
The City of *London*, having petition'd the Houfe
againft Sir *George Jeffereys* their Recorder, and it
being referr'd to a Committee, they pafs'd this
Vote on the 13th of *November* following,

" *Refolv'd*, That this Committee is of opinion,
" That by the Evidence given to this Commit-
" tee, it does appear that Sir *George Jeffereys*, Re-
" corder of the City of *London*, by traducing and
' obftructing Petitioning for the fitting of this Par-
' liament, hath betrayed the Rights of the Subject.
To which the Houfe agreed, and 'twas order'd,
" That an humble Addrefs be made to his Majefty
" to remove him out of all publick Offices ".
They farther Order'd likewife, That the Committee fhould enquire into all fuch perfons as had
been advifing or promoting of the late Proclamation, ftiled, *A Proclamation againft Tumultuous
Petitioning*   The Grand Juries of the Counties of
Somerfet and *Devon* having expreffed their Detefta-
tion of fuch Petitioning, the Houfe on the nine-
teenth of *November* order'd that the two Foremen
of the faid Juries, and two others, fhould be fent
for in Cuftody of the Serjeant at Arms, to anfwer
for Breach of Privilege (as they called this Ab-

H   hor-

horrence of Petitioning) by them committed a
gainst the House The next d. they voted, Th..
one *Thomas Herbert* Esq should . sent for in Cu
stody, for profecuting *John Arnold* Esq, at the
Council Table, for *promoting a Petition and pro
curing Subfcriptions* To them they added two o
thers upon the fame account, whom they call'd,
Betrayers of the Liberties of the Subject

Anfwer

*Meafures were not taken to run down the Right
tle Subject, but to affert that of the Prince, wo
was of too gracious a Nature to tl nft after an Ex
orbitancy of Power, and of too Fatherly a Difpofi
tion, not to have a tender regard for the Welfare o
his People , and an Impartial Enquiry will infor
us, that the Cry of the Houfe at that time was again
every one that was in Favour of his Prince as a* Be
trayer of his Country, *and an Enemy to that fort
of Government they were defirous of introducing* S
that its no wonder that Sir George Jeffereys, *fo
advifing the Citizens, as it was his Duty*, not to Pe
tition, *and Sir* Francis Wythens, *for his Abhor
rence of* Tumultuary Proceedings, *fell under ti.
high Difpleafure of the Houfe* But I cannot but tak
*notice that the Houfe in thofe Times of Reform
tion imprifon'd (that is, order'd Mr* Herbert *in
Cuftod) one that was not a Member, which is a fuffi
cient Precedent for what has been done of the fame na
ture in this Parliament*

On *Wednefday* the fifth of *January*, the Com
mons order'd an Impeachment againft Sir *Fran
cis North*, Chief Juftice of the *Common Pleas* , Su
William Scroggs, Chief Juftice of the *Kings Bench*,
Sir *Thomas Jones*, one of the Juftices of the fame
Bench, and Sir *Richard Wefton*, one of the Barons of the *Exchequer* Sir *Francis North*'s Crime
was, That he (as appear'd by the Confeffion of
the

Attorney-General before the Houſe on *Wedneſday*
the 4th of *November*) w..s, *Adv ſing and aſſiſting
in drawing up and pcſſing the Pi oclamations againſt
Tumultuous Petitions* Againſt Sir *William Scroggs*
and Sir *Thomas Jones* there were a great many
Complaints, which occaſion'd many Reſolutions
of the Houſe, and Votes againſt them One of
the great Complaints was, That when the Grand-
Juiy which ſerv'd for the Hundred cf *Oſſulſton*
in the County of *Middleſex*, attended the *Kings-
Bench* with a Petition, which they deſir'd the
Court to preſent in their Name to his Majeſty,
for the ſitting ot that Parliament, the Chief Juſtice ſaid, he would diſpatch them preſently;
That they took it ill to have a Petition ofter'd to
alter the King's Mind contrary to his Proclamation, That when there were ſeveral Preſent-
ments aginſt Papiſts and other Offenders, they
diſcharg'd the Grand Jury four days before the
erd of the Term, which was never done before
This Act they voted *Arbitrary, Illegal, and a high
Miſdemeanour*, ſeveral days before this Impeachment was order'd. One of Mr Baron *Weſton's*
great Crimes was, That, in an extraoidinary
kind of Charge given the Aſſizes before at *King-
ſton* (in the County of *Surrey*) he inveigh'd very
much againſt *Fuel, Luther, Calvin* and *Zuinglius*,
condemning them as Authors of the Reformation Which was aginſt their Princes Minds, and
then adding to this purpoſe *Zuinglius ſet up his
Fanaticiſm, and Calvin built on that bleſſed Foundation and to ſpeak Truth, all his Diſciples aie ſea-
ſon'd with ſuch a ſharpneſs of Spirit, that it much
concerns Magiſtrates to keep a ſtreight hand over them,
and now they aie reſtleſs, amuſing us with Fears,
AND NOTHING WILL SERVE THEM
BUT A PARLIAMENT For my part, I
know no Repreſentative of the Nation but the KING,
all Power centeis in Him* 'Tis true, he does intruſt it

witL

*with his Miniflers, but he is the fole Reprefentative ,
and i'faith he has Wifdom enough to intruft it no more
in thefe Men. who have given us fuch late Examples
of their Wifdom and Faithfulnefs.* Thefe Words
(which were witneffed by feveral perfons, fome of
whom put them immediately in writing) made
the Committee before whom they were prov'd
come to this Refolution, " That the faid Expref-
" fions in the Charge given by the faid Baron
" *Weflon*, were a Scandal to the Reformation, in
" derogation of the Rights and Privileges of Par-
" liaments, and tending to raife Difcord between
" his Majefty and his Subjects.

Anfwer.

*Their Impeachment of the Judges is much of the
fame Complexion with their Treatment of thofe laft
mentioned, and Petitions againft Proclamations look
fo very like a Defiance of the Defigns of 'em, that it
was wholly neceffary to fupprefs 'em, in order to keep
the Publick Peace. But we have a more clear Indication of their Tempers as well as Religion, from their
Vote,* That it was a Scandal to the Reformation *for
Mr Baron* Weflon *to call* Zuinglius *his Principles*
Fanaticifms, *and to fay* Calvin *and* Luther *built
upon the fame bleffed Foundation, fince they were
altogether very diftant from the Articles of Religion
profefs'd in the Church of* England *by Law eftablifhed.*

Two days after that the Commons agreed upon Impeaching thefe Great Men of the Law (who
every one came under the publick Cenfure for
appearing *Abhorrers* of Petitioning for the Sitting of
the Parliament) they fell into other Votes, which
fhew'd what it was they wanted a Parliament
for Upon a Meffage fent to them from his Majefty, they came to thefe feveral Refolutions following

" *Refolv'd,*

" *Refolv'd*, That it is the Opinion of this Houfe,
" That there is no Security or Safety for the Pro-
" teftant Religion, the King's Life, or the Well-
" conftituted and Eftablifh'd Government of this
" Kingdom, without pafling a Bill for Difabling
" *James* Duke of *York* to inherit the Imperial
" Crown of *England* and *Ireland*, and the Domini-
" ons and Territories thereunto belonging And
" to rely upon any other Means or Remedies
" without fuch a Bill, is not only infufficient, but
" dangerous.

" *Refolv'd*, That his Majefty in his laft Meffage
" having affur'd this Houfe of his Readinefs to
" concur in all other Means for the Prefervation of
" the Proteftant Religion, this Houfe doth de-
" clare, That until a Bill be likewife pafs'd for
" Excluding the Duke of *York*, this Houfe can-
" not give any Supply to his Majefty, with-
" out Danger to his Majefty's Perfon, extreme
" Hazard of the Proteftant Religion, and Unfaith-
" fulnefs to thofe by whom this Houfe is en-
" trufted.

" *Refolv'd*, That all Perfons who advis'd his
" Majefty in his laft Meffage to this Houfe, to in-
" fift upon an Opinion againft the Bill for Exclu-
" ding the Duke of *York*, have given pernicious
" Councel to his Maiefty, and are P R O M O-
" T E R S O F P O P É R Y, A N D E N E-
" M I E S T O T H E K I N G A N D KING-
" D O M.

After thefe General Refolutions, they ran into
fevere Votes and Refolutions againft *Geo--ge* E of
Hal---x, *H--ry* Mar--qs of *Wor---er*, *H---ry* E. of
Cla---on, *Law---ce H-de* Efq, *Le--s* E of *Fev---am*.
A Motion was alfo made for an Addrefs to his
Majefty to remove *Ed--rd Sey--r* Efq, from his
Majefty's Council and Prefence, but it was ad-
journ'd to the *Monday* following, which was the
day on which the Parliament was prorogu'd.

'The

The reafon perhaps why they did not prefs this Motion, was becaufe they had agreed upon Articles of Impeachment againft him, upon other fcores, juft twenty days before

Anfwer

After they had, as it were, quarrell'd with their God, in the Vindication of falfe Doctrines, and what was diffonant to the Liturgy of thefe Nations, it was but natural for 'em to fall upon their Prince, and wound his Honour in the Perfon of his Royal Brother and Succeffor. The Bill of Exclufion was a thing to be agreed upon in return to His Majefty's mcft gracious Meffage, and the celebrated Names that bear the Royal Unfortunate Company, amongft whom is the pre-fent Earl of Rochefter *, now Lord Lieutenant of* Ireland*, and his prefent Majefty's Uncle and Councelloi, were to be Sharers with him in his Misfortunes and the Lofs of his Inheritance* Oh the Effrontery ' *(to make ufe of his own words) none but a* Calvinift *would write in behalf of fuch fhamelefs Endeazours, and none but a murmuring* Puritan *would defend 'em*

Their warm Proceedings, and their infifting upon that particular Method to fecure the Proteftant Religion, occafion'd not only the Prorogation of this Parliament on the 10th of *January*, but of the following Parliament likewife at *Oxford*, which met the 21ft of *March*, and was difmifs'd on the 28th as foon as they read the Bill of Exclufion brought in there On the 10th of *January* the Houfe of Commons knowing that they were to be prorogu'd, before the Prorogation came to feveral Refolut ons, two of which I fhall here take notice of.

     " *Refolv'd*,

1 " *Refolv'd,* That whofoever advis'd his Ma-
" jefty to prorogue this Parliament to any other
" purpofe than in order to the pailing of a Bill for
" the Exclufion of *James* Duke of *York*, is a Betray-
" er of the King, the Proteftant Religion, and of
" the Kingdom of *England,* A P R O M O T E R
" O F T H E *FRENCH* I N T E R E S T,
" AND A PENSIONER TO *FRANCE.*
2 " *Refolv'd,* That the Thanks of this Houfe
" be given to the C I T Y O F *L O N D O N,* for
" their manifeft Loyalty to the King, their Care,
" Charge, and Vigilance for the Prefervation of
" his Majefty's Perfon, and of the Proteftant Reli-
" gion " This Care and Concern which the City
of *London* fhew'd for the Proteftant Religion, in
that time of imminent Danger, appear'd in many
Inftances, and in two particularly, which the Houfe
thought did then deferve a grateful Acknowledgement, firft in petitioning the King for the Sitting
of that Parliament , fecondly, in voting an Addrefs to his Majefty to declare their Loyalty , and
to petition him that the Parliament might fit until
Proteftantifm was fecur'd.

Anfwer.

Their warm Proceedings *in thofe days were not fo
much the effect of their Zeal for the Proteftant Religion,
as their Hatred for the Perfon of the Duke of* York,
*who, if any thing could have gain'd upon their Refent-
ments, or abated their Difpleafure, was at that time
accounted one of the fineft Princes in* Europe, (*not-
withftanding his late Degeneracy) and had done things
for the Publick Service, which had the Acknowledgments
of all Chriftian Princes, and would have work'd upon
any bodies Temper, but the minds of fome men that
were prejudic'd and embitter'd againft him And the
two* Refolutions, *One of Cenfure, by which we may
fee they were of the fame* Stamp *with fome that would
govern in the* Houfe *now, from their being faid to*

P R O-

(56)

PROMOTE THE *FRENCH* INTE.
REST, *as* PENSIONERS TO *FRANCE*,
while they were serving their Country , and the Other
of Thanks, by way of Acknowledgment to the City of
London, *for their great Loyalty to the King, while*
they were excluding his only Brother from his Right of
Inheritance, and the care they had for the Security of
Proteſtantiſm, *at the ſame time as Defamatory Pi-*
&ures and Libels were handed about to traduce the
Hierarchy, and depretiate the Eſteem which was had
for the Sacred Order of Biſhops. Thanks be to God,
the Tide is turn'd once more in our days, and honeſt
Men have the ſatisfaƈtion of ſeeing a Majority in the
Court of Aldermen that are true Sons to the Church of
England, *and the Lieutenancy in all probability will*
in due time be ſo ſettled, that it may be ſaid of our
London *Epiſcopal Churches,* The Gates of Hell
ſhall not prevail againſt 'em.

Having given this Account of the Proceedings
both of the Courtiers and Houſe of Commons, the
one to run down, the other to aſſert the Subjeƈts
Right of Petitioning in thoſe days I muſt crave
leave to take notice of what paſſed afterwards, becauſe 'twill be of uſe to us in the matter I am
now treating of.

After the Diſſolution of the *Oxford* Parliament,
the King publiſh'd a Declaration , wherein he
vouchſaf'd *to declare the Cauſes and Reaſons of his*
Aƈtions to his People It might very well be imagin'd, that after the People had ſo univerſally petition'd for a Sitting of the laſt Parliament at *Weſt-*
minſter , to ſecure their Religion and Liberties,
which the Conſpirators were now attacking with
the utmoſt vigor, they were more than a little a-
larum'd to ſee that and the ſucceeding Parliament
at *Oxford* ſo ſoon diſſolv'd, and that deny'd them
which they thought the only Security for their
Religion. He begins therefore with telling them,

That

That 'twas *with exceeding great trouble that he was
brought to dissolve the two last Parliaments* 'Twere
well that those who in their Votes concerning the
Kentish Petition, shew'd that they have not forgotten the Spirit of the Court at that time, as
to their Abhorrence of Petitioning, had remember'd their other Resentments, express'd in this
Declaration, as the Reasons for Dissolving that
Parliament

Answer.

*His Majesty, as a Wise and Indulgent Prince, that
had a Fatherly Concern for his People, and a Tender-
ness of Nature that was deriv'd from that August
Family which he ow'd his Being to, was loth that his
Subjects should interpret his Actions otherwise than
they were design'd, and put an evil Construction on
what was intended to promote the Publick Tranquility. He therefore issued out his Reasons by way of
Proclamation, and the indispensable Necessity he lay
under of Dissolving that Parliament, that so* despight-
fully *used the Royal Authority, and set at nought
the Desires and Requests of God's Anointed, and what
was urged in behalf of his Proceedings, carry'd such
convincing Proofs with it, at the time of its being
made Publick, that it settled the Minds of those that
were wavering in their Duties, and was attended with
such good Effects, that* Addresses *came to his sacred hands
instead of* insolent Petitions, *and the most thinking
part of the World was satisfied from his Majest'ys
Actions that he postpon'd his own Profit to their Advantage and Ease.*

I   One

One Complaint is, That the *Commons made arbitary illegal Orders, fer taking Perfons into Cuftody
for matters that had no relation to Privilege of Parliament* Was it at that time arbitrary and illegal to take thofe degenerate Wretches into Cuftody, who publifh'd under their Hands Abhorrences of Parliaments, and of thofe who in humble
and lawful Manner petitioned for their Sitting
in a time of fuch extream Neceffity, and is it
not now fo to imprifon and confine Men for
doing their Duty to their King and Country, no
otherwife than the Law prefcribes ? Is it a greater Breach of Privilege to fhew a Letter written
by Sir *Ed --d Se----r*, then, in compliance with
a ftrange arbitary illegal Proclamation, to run
down the Subjeĉt's Right of Petitioning, and
thus, in effeĉt, to ftrike at Parliaments them
felves, and endeavour to wound the Conftitution ?
What would Mr *Bo - n* have faid to this ? Sure
ly he muft have blufh'd to fee his old Friends,
whofe Intereft he then ferv'd, in running down
the *Commons* Power of imprifoning, exercife fuch
Aĉts of Power as were never heard of in *England*
before *Tom Sheridan*, who labour'd in the fame
Caufe, and wrote againft that Power of the *Commons*, which he felt in his own Perfon, with as
much Warmth as 'twas poffible for *Bo-- n* to do,
did he fee thefe things, wou'd be able perhaps, to
behold them wi h little aftonifhment He knew
the Frailty of Human Nature, and carried much
of it about in his own Body, for after he had
taken a great deal of Pains (as alfo the Royal
Scribes of thofe times, and his Religion did) in
decrying *Fanatic fm* and *Republican* Principles, in
crying up Epifcopacy and the Church of *England*
and refcuing the Minds of Men from thofe
groundlefs Fears of Popery, which were running
them into Meafures pernicious to the *Duke* his
Mafter s

Master's Interest, he saw, poor Man, Popery rampant, and a Popish King in *England*, he saw the Bishops, and (which he could not but wonder at) was glad to see them, in the Tower, and, which must be the greatest wonder of all to such a zealous Churchman as he was, he saw himself a Papist It wou'd therefore be now the less surprising to him to see his old loyal Friends turn'd downright Republicans, and as violent in the House of *Commons* for illegal and arbitrary imprisoning, as they were against that, and all other Power in the Commons.

Answer.

The Complaint had all manner of Justice in its side, since it was certainly a diminution of the Regal Authority, and destructive of the King's Prerogative, to imprison those faithful and affectionate Subjects, that had made a tender to him of their Allegiance and Services, and the Declaration *could not be illegal, since it was His* Majesty's Right *to issue it forth, nor arbitrary, because it contain'd nothing in it that promoted such violent Methods, and was the result of the King's Will and* Pleasure, *in conjunction with the Advice of his* Privy Council, *according to Form, and the standing Rules of the Land therefore the compliance with it could not wound the Constitution, or strike at the Honour of* Parliaments, *when the ill Offices that were done to Sir* Edward Seymour *in relation to the Letter he makes mention, was a manifest Breach of Privilege, and highly injurious to the Dignity those he represented had intrusted him with the preservation of*

Another

Another Complaint in the *Declaration*, and a
R_afon given for diffolv_ing thofe Parliaments, is
th_ir *ftrange illegal Votes, decla_ing divers eminent*
Perfons to be Enemies to the King and Kingdom,
and d_fi_ing to have t_em remov'd from the King's
Council and Prefence, without any Orde_ or Procefs of
Law, a_y Hearing of their Def_nce, o_ any Proof fo
much as offe_d ag_ainft them The Perfons he_e
po_nted at in the Decla_ation are very w_ell know_n,
fo is the Cr_me for w_hich th_y a_e D_clar'd Enemies to *t_e King and Kingdom* T_m_ h_s fhe_n
whether thof_ P_rl_amen_s h_d r_afo_n to e_prefs
their Refentm_nts aga_nft _h_t M_n_ ho _dher_d
to the Duke of *Y__k's* In_r__t Had _h_y be_n
lefs warm for h_m, th_y h_d p_rha_p_ be_n k_nd
_er to their Religion and Co_n_ry '_I_s c_rta_n
that extraord_nary Art_hc__ _ere made _fe of to
fupport h_r Intereft Such I m_y c_ll this ver
Declarat_ion, which thought it was r_ckon'd fo_
very good Re_fon_, to be con_riv'd by a gr_at
French M_n_lter, tho _t came not ou_ unde_ the
Great S_al, and was onl_ fub_crib_d by *F_ancis*
Gwyn the Cl_rk of th_ Coun_l yet was read pub
l_ckl_ _n the Chu_ch_s Such I m_y reckon the
A_drefs s contr_v d and fent up b_ Men of the
fame Le_en w_th the form_r *Ab_o_ _s* W_herein
fome _f__be__ to h_s M_j_ ,'s _f fdom _n_ So_e_a_g_
_iu_l_____, that we ar_ not relapfing __to t_e M_je
r_es _n_ c_n_j_ar__ _f 1_r_n_ an_ C_ar_ation, __
t_e f_lt_ _n _f__ a_d Cu_n_g Contr_v__nces of t__
old *ENEMILS O_ THE MON_ARCHY_AND*
TH_ CH_RCH Others, In_t _t _s t_e K_n_
a_m's Int_r_ff __c _ _u_ _e t_e S_r_ff on _n _ts _u_ a _
r_g'_ L_r_, _nd ta_e upon th_m to th_nk his Ma
j_fty, f_r _s _ r__r_ble R_fo__ _ to pr_fe_ve th_
C_c_n _n __ lu_ c_ _ _t_at _c__ _f D_f_n_, and un
d_r__ke to fr__ F__ _'_ L_c__ _n pr_r_ve t_e K_n_
H_rs _u__r_ s__f__ A_d _ _c tr__ L_e
_n_

and Fortunes to *his Majesty's dispofal for this purpose.*
It must be astonishing as well as surprising in those
Days, that when Petitions had been not only dif-
countenanc'd, but forbidden by *Proclamations, Addresses* should so soon after be encourag'd and promoted, especially when we consider that the
Petitions were in reference to matters which
every Body understood, and in relation to things
wherein the Law justified the Petitioners Whereas Addresses respected Matters which very few
understood, and which the Law no way authori-
les private Men to meddle with, and which none
save a Parliament have Power to decide or determine. If change of Parties in St *Stephens Chappel*
make it not astonishing to us now to see a *H----se*
of Com - s treat Gentlemen so severely as this has
done for presenting a legal Petition, when another
House has called others to account for expressing
their Abhorrence of Petitioning, yet it must
seem a little strange, to see those who promoted
Addresses to the King to secure the Interest of a
Popish Successor, imprison so many Gentlemen of
Worth and Note in their Country, for addressing
them and praying in the most difficult Times we
ever fell into, that our Religion and Safety may
effectually be provided for, and that a King, who
under God has preserv'd the Protestant Religion,
may be enabled to assist his allies, and consequently
preserve our Religion and Liberties But if nothing of this be strange, is it not a little amazing
to compare some Mens Proceedings against o-
thers, with those Remonstrances to the Nation
publish'd in the Houses of God, where they complain of *Eminent Persons being voted Enemies to the*
King and Kingdom, and addressed against to have
them remov'd from the *King's Council and Presence,*
without any Ordar or Process of Law, any Hearing of
their Defence Were such Votes and Addresses
greater Hardships in the Reign of a King who
                                                     made

made it his Rule to heap Favours on thofe who
were under the Difpleafure of the Houfe of Commons, than they are under a Prince, whom the
Commons reckon oblig'd in a manner to comply
with them in all their Defires ?

Anfwer

*Tho' it could not be arbitrary in the King to iffue
forth a* Declaration *according to Law,* 'twas *a high
Prefumption in the Subject to declare divers* Eminent
Perfons *to be* Enemies to the King and Kingdom,
*&c for adhering only to His Majefty's Intereft, and
the* due Succeffion *of the Royal Family* The Cafe
of thofe Noble Peers *was hugely diftant from that
of the* Lords *lately Impeached, who had Articles in
due Form and Courfe exhibited againft* 'em *for high
Crimes and* real *Mifdemeanours, not thofe that were
fictitious, and not profecuted for want of Evidence ,
and any one that has any remembrance of King*
CHARLES *the Second, and calls to mind his
Clearnefs of Wit, and Vivacity of Expreffion, can
never think he ftood in need of a* French Orator *to
dictate to him, or a* Foreign Amanuenfis *to put
his Words in due Form for him As for the Charge
he lays upon thofe Worthy Gentlemen who could not
have committed the* Kentifh Petitioners *without a
Majority, I dare affirm that* Ten of 'em *never fate
in the* Oxford Parliament, *and if the* Commons
of England *have oblig'd his prefent Majefty in the
Grant of* All, *at leaft the* Chiefeft *of his Defires,
it is but a* reciprocal Obligation *that lies upon
Him to gratifie them with a Compliance to their
Requefts, that are not actrimental to his* Kingly
Authority

From

From what I have ſaid it appears when, and upon what account the Subject's Right of Petitioning was run down As the Petitions offer'd by the People were for the Sitting of the Parliament, and that, to have their Religion and Liberty ſecur'd in a time of great and manifeſt Danger So were the *Abhorrences* of thoſe Petitions ſet a foot, four Parliaments diſſolv'd, the King's *Declaration* containing the Reaſon of it publiſh'd in Churches, and the *Thanksgiving Addreſſes* to his majeſty afterwards procur'd to defeat the Meaſures then taken for the Preſervation of our Religion and to ſecure the Duke of *York*'s peaceable Succeſſion to the Crown If there be any who conſider, That thoſe who have a concern for the Proteſtant Religion, muſt apprehend at leaſt as much Evil from K J or his Family's returning now, as from his Succeſſion at that time, and that as it is of as great Importance to the Affairs of *France* to have him on the Throne, or Confuſion in England, as then it was, ſo Count Ta---rd muſt be as induſtrious in taking Meaſures to ſerve his Maſter, as Mr. *Bar-..-on* was in thoſe Days It muſt be a very melancholy Reflection to them, to think how differing the Temper of the Co--- us of *England* now is from what it was then And to ſee the Power in their Hands, who were in all thoſe Court-meaſures which, I'm afraid, have not yet had their worſt Effects.

.   Anſwer

The Commons *of* England *have acted this laſt Seſſions ſo little favourably to* King James *his Intereſt* *, that howſoever induſtrious* Count Tallard *might be for His and his Maſter's Service, he met with very ill Succeſs , which convinces me that he was not ſo laviſh of his* Louis d'Ors *as our Author*
wou'd

would intimate, who seems to be altogether in the
dark, and as foreign from the knowledge of that
Minister's Golden Negotiations, as any man
breathing And the King of France has other Fish
to fry in the Spanish Territories about the Succeſſion,
than to be at liberty at this time to aſſert a Prince's
Title he has already relinquiſh'd in the late Articles of
Peace, and dec ai'd to be of no Force by his owning
King William Monſieur Barillon's Induſtry to
ferve his Maſter was at a time when the eyes of all
our Europe were fix'd on the Inclination of this
Court, and other Princes waited to take their Meaſures
from the Diſcoveries that could be made of which
ſide England would take, that of France or Spain
and the French Miniſter of a later date employ'd his
Artifices to bring over ſome Courtiers to his ſide, who
were neither honeſt enough to reſiſt Temptations, nor
had Love enough to their Prince and Country, not
to forward the Intereſt of another Monarch by the
Treaty of Partition But as for Engagements made
with Senators, or Gifts diſtributed to ai an over the
Country Party to his Maſter's ſide, not a Reſolution
made during this whole Seſſion of Parliament has
given the leaſt grounds for ſuch a Suſpicion, but on
the contrary, has made appear to all Chriſtendom
that the Exorbitant Greatneſs of France was an Eye-
ſore to them, and they unanimouſly voted ſuch Meaſures to be taken as might ſtrengthen our Alliance
with our old Friend and Confederate the Emperour,
and in Conjunction with the States of Holland, enable
him to make good his Pretenſions to the Dominions
of Spain, which had been in the Auſtrian Family for ſome Ages, and were fraudulently uſurp'd
by a Young Prince of the Houſe of Bourbon

Good

Good-natur'd People, who are as far from being fuspicious of others, as they are from evil Defigns themfelves, do, I know, judge thofe Men too fevere in their Cenfures, who think that in the Tieatment of the *Kentifh* Petitioners there were the fame Regaids and Defigns that were formerly in their *Abhorrences* and *Addreffes* Or that this was done to giatify Count *Ta---rd*, and, by ftriking a Terior, to prevent the People from running univerfally into Petitions and Addreffes, and conjuring up a Spirit in the Nation which might be very prejudicial to his Mafters Affairs. 'Tis true indeed, they do, and muft own, that 'tis haid to account for the Severity of their Proceedings: That when the Law has in expiefs Words provided that People may petition the Parliament, they fhou'd place fuch an Affront on the County of *Kent* (I fhou'd fay the whole Kingdom of *England*) and to imprifon their Delegates after the mannei they did. If every Part of the *Petition* was not fo nicely worded as they wou'd have it, wou'd it not be fufhcient to reprove them for it ? Wou'd no lefs Punifhment than Imprifonment do? If any of their own Members be at any time tax'd for fpeaking amifs, they are fuffer'd to explain themfelves, why fhould not they allow otheis to do the fame? If there was any thing in the Petition which the Houfe thought a Reflection, one of the Gentlemen told Sir *The--us Ogl--rp*, they wou'd declare at the Bar of the Houfe that 'twas what they did not defign, and wou'd ask Pardon for it, but nothing wou'd ferve that Plenipotentiary's turn but to have them declare that they were forry for prefenting the Petition, which they never wou'd do

Anfw *Whatever he means by* good-natur'd People, *it is not my Bufinefs to explain, but I dare*

K *affirm*

affirm that any Person of less Simplicity than a mere Natural, *with half an Eye can find out the same Pernicious Designs, as were in the Petitions to* King Charles *the First, and might have had the same Consequences in creating a Misunderstanding between* King *and* People, *had not the Prudence of our Senators timely prevented the spreading of the Disease, like Skilful Surgeons that make use of Painful Remedies, such as Amputations to stop the Progress of the* Gangrene--- Ne pars sincera trahatur, *left it should diffuse it self amidst the Vitals, and occasion the Death of their Patient. The Abhorrences in* King Charles *the* 2d s *Time did not aim at the Diminution* (or rather Suppression) *of the Legislative Authority, but were for the Advancement and Increase of it, they made the Prosperity of the King, the Success of the People, and interwove the Prerogative with the Immunities of the Subject ; when that which is now brought as an Instance before us was for placing the whole Authority in the People that sent it, and impudently assum'd the Liberty of* Advising *those whom they should* seek Advice *from, as they did in a manner declare War, and cry out,* To your Tents, O Israel. *Now the Question is, whether Count* Talard's *Louis d' O'rs had taken their Progress into* Kent, *instead of making a Visit to St* Stephen's, Chappel *(as our Author would perswade the World) for it's as clear as the Light it self, to be the only way to set the* Nation *together by the* Ears *and create Intestine Divisions, was to advance a Proposition that one Third of 'em did not think advisable for their Safety ; and* found the Trumpet *for a* War, *when they were yet languishing under the Effects of it, and were so far from being recover'd to their former State of Health by a* Peace, *that the present Tranquility we enjoy, must have some Years continuance before we can be perfectly able to tast the Sweets of it.*

That

That which gave offence was, calling
then *Addreffes Loyal*: If they were *Loyal,*
it cou'd be no Reflection to call them fo; if
they were not, they had Reafon I confefs 'to
think it a Jeer, and at the fame time they ought
to confefs that 'twas what they deferv'd It is
moft certain, that the Defign of the Gentlemen
who fign'd that Petition, was to ferve their
Country by it, which they did effectually: the
Methods then that they made ufe of muft be
fuch as they thought propereft for that end ;
wherefore the Goodnefs and Sincerity of their
Intentions muft filence every thing that can be
faid againft then way of exprefling themfelves.

Anfw. *Men are apt to make a Judgment of the*
Sincerity *of People's* Intentions *from their Expreffions, and where* undutiful *Words are made
ufe of, there, we may prefume, are fome Defigns of
falling from* Obedience. *The Epithet* LOYAL
was given to the Parliament Addreffes by way of
IRONY, *not as if they were not actually fo, and
fhew'd the Defign of the* Kentifh *Petitioners was to
defame 'em, by faying as much as, their* Hearts
were open and ready to make His Majefty a
Tender of their Obedience, but their Purfes
were fhut, and contradicted their fair Speeches
by refufing to give him Affiftance. *If this be
not an indecent Reflection upon the Honour of Parliaments, let the Pamphleteer tell me what is, and
if he can produce an Inftance of fo contumacious a
Nature amidft any of thofe Reverential* Addreffes
which he call's Abhoriences, *I'll fairly own my
felf in the wrong, and fubfcribe to the Truth of
what he lays down for unqueftionable Verity.*

The Cenfure of the Commons is very fevere,
they tell us the Petition is *fcandalous, infolent,
feditious, tending to deftroy the Conftitution of Parliament, and fubvert the eftablifh'd Government of
this Realm.* By the Harfhnefs of the Expreflions,

a

a Man wou'd think that this Petition were an
Addrefs to a King, or a *Remonftrance* that
chaig'd him with a *felonious Confpiracy*, oi
making a *Treaty in its own Nature unjuft* How
can it be *fcandalous* or *infolent* for fo confiderable a Branch of the *Englifh* Nation to prefent
an humble Petition to their *Delegates*, and pray
their *Attorneys* (as *Members* weie formeily
call'd) to take care of the Bufinefs they intruft-
ed them with? How can it be *fed'tious* to fhew
an extraordinary and unparalleli'd Zeal for the
King, to pray that he may be enabled to *affift his Allies*, and that *God may long continue his
propitious and unblemifh'd Reign over us*? How
can it *tend to deftroy the Conftit tion of Parliament,
and fubvert the eftablifh'd Government of th s
Realm*, to piay to have thofe things done,
which aie abfolutely neceffary to prevent our
falling into the hands of thofe Enemies who
will ceitainly deftroy the *Conftitution of Parl a-
ment*, and *fubvert the eftablifh d Govei ment of
th s Re lm* The laft *Weftminfter* Parliament in
the Reign of K *Charles* II Refolv'd, *Nem ne
Con'radicente*, (as I obferv d be'oie) *That o
traduce Petitioning as a Violation of Duty, and to
reprefent it to his Majefty as tumultuous and fe-
dtious, is to betray the Liberty of the Subject, and
cont ibute, to the Defign of fubverting the artic,
leg il Conftitution of this Kingdom, and introduci g
Arbitrary Powei* This Parliament iefolves, that
the *Kertifh* Petition tends *to deftroy the Con-
ftitut on of Parliament, and to fubveit the eftablifhed Government of this Realm*. 'Tis very ftiange
that to *traduce Petitioning*, and to *petition* fhou'd
both tend to fubveit the Conftitution.

Anfw The *Refolution of the Commons in Refe
re ce to the Petition was fo neceffary at that jun-
Eure, that it could not be tax'd with Severity,
fince it prevented the Nation from entring into
Pic.*

*Plots and Parties, and confederating for each o-
thers imaginary Security, and the Expreffions in it
are much more unblameable, than what was made ufe
of in the Remonftrance it Cenfur'd, and the County of* Kent *have made themfelves fo* Inconfidera-
ble a Part of the Nation *by the Prefc tment of it,
that it was requifite thofe Gentlemen who reprefent-
ed the* Whole *fhou'd let 'em know it. It's a war-
rantable thing to pray for his Majefty, but it s
certainly unjuft and unmannerly to revile the Reprefentatives of his Subjects, it cannot be feditious
to fend up Entreaties to Heaven to preferve the eftablifh'd Government, but it looks like fomething of
the fame mutirous Complexior, to give Hints in a
Petition as if it were in danger, and difquiet the
Minds of the People by acquainting 'em, that
Matters were not fairly carried, when the Seffion
has concluded with all imaginable Advantage to the
Publick, by the Prudent Management of our Wife
Reprefentatives.*

If it be the undouoted Right of the Sub;ect to
petition, 'twill be very eafy to determin which
of the two *Refolutions* is righteft, and if we com-
p_re the former Inclinations of a Party with their
late Proceedings, 'twill be evident to us, how
the laft *Refol tion* happens to be wrong. But
'tis faid that there is fome thing particular in
the *Petition,* which juftifies this *Refolution*, the
Petition directs the Houfe of Commons, and
tells them what they fhall do, this, they fay,
is infolent, and *tends to deftroy the Conftitution of
Parliament, and to fubvert the eftablifh d Government of this Realm.* Very ftrange! Can any
Man or Body of Men order a Petition to o hers,
that is not liable to the fame Cenfure? Does
not their Petitioning plainly fay, that they
think themfelves aggriev d? Does not their
Prayer direct thofe to whom they addrefs, what
they are to do? But how this *Petition* of the
Grand

Grand Jury, Juſtices of Peace, and Freeholders of the County of *Kent,* can be ſaid to *tend to deſtroy the Conſtitution of Parliament, and to ſubvert the eſtabliſh'd Government of this Realm,* is to me very difficult to conceive.

Anſw. *It's the Subjects undoubted Right to* Petition, *but not to make uſe of Words that ſhew him Superior to the Power he makes Addreſs to, and derogate from their Authority whom he begs Aſſiſtance from   They were not Impriſon'd for* Petitioning, *but taking the Poſts of thoſe Gentlemen the Petition was given to, and Uſurping a* Freedom of Speech *which is not Tolerated in any Perſon that is not a Member of that Venerable Aſſembly   If their Repreſentatives were not Wiſer than themſelves, Why did they Chuſe 'em ? If they were not above being Directed, and Capable of making Proviſion for the Security of the Publick, Why were they Entruſted with the Preſervation of their Liberties and all that was Valuable to Men, as Rational Creatures ?*

Had this indeed, which is an humble *Petition,* carry'd Authority and Power in it, had they pretended to a Right to command the Houſe of Commons to do what they would have them, I cannot ſee how even ſuch an aſſuming Addreſs as this cou'd bring our Conſtitution into any great hazard. Shou'd the whole Freeholders of the County of *Kent* join unanimouſly in ſuch an Addreſs, yet wou'd the *Power* and *Authority* of the Repreſentatives of the Freemen of *England,* and the *Conſtitution of Parliament,* reſt very ſecure in the Judgment of the reſt of the People, who wou'd never juſtify ſuch an Uſurp'd Authority   An uſurp'd Authority I call it, and muſt ſubſcribe to that, as what I take to be very moderate and juſt, which Colonel *Algernon Sidney* ſays in that Diſcourſe which coſt him his Life ; *I believe, may be, that the Powers of every County, City and Bor*

Borough of England, *are regulated by the General Law to which they have all consented, and by
which they are all made Members of one Political
Body---Among us every County does not make a di-
stinct Body, having in it self a Sovereign Power,
but is a Member of that great Body wh:ch compre-
hends the whole Nation* 'Tis *not therefore for*
KENT *or* SU?SEX, LEWIS *or* MAIDSTONE,
*but for the whole Nation that the Members chosen
in those Places are sent to serve in Parliament.
And tho' it be fit for them as Friends and Neighbours (so far as may be) to hearken to the Opini-
ons of the Electors for the Information of their
Judgments, and to the end that what they shall say
may be of more weight, when every one is known not
to speak his own Thoughts only, but those of a great
Number of Men, yet they are not strictly and pro-
perly oblig'd to give account of their Actions to any,
unless the whole Body of the Nation for wh.ch they
serve, and who are equally co-cern'd in their Reso-
lutions, cou'd be assembl'd. This be ing impractic-
ble, the only Punishment to which they are subject,
if they betray their Trust, is* SCORN, INFAMY,
HATRED, AND , N ASSURANCE OF BE-
ING REJECTED WHEN THEY SHALL A-
GAIN SEEK THE SAME HONOUR

An'w. *But suppose this* Humble Petition *af-
sum'd a Power which did not belong to Petitioners
(as it actually did) where was the fault of suppres-
sing it ? Suppose it had no such thing as* Humility
*in it, but on the contrary was Arrogant and Pre-
sumptuous, and tended to the creation of Jealousies,
amongst his Majesty's good Subjects, why should it
not be said* to tend to destroy the Constitution of
Parliaments, and to subvert the establish'd Government of this Realm ? *What has been done,
may be done again, and there are some living that
have seen a Civil War spring from the same Beginnings, and can witness such Humble Proceedings*

*as these have occasion'd such Insolence as is not to be
Parallell'd in History, and such disrespect to Crown'd
Head , as to Condemn Sacred Majesty as the Vilest
Criminal, and turn Decency and Order into the
greatest Confusion As for Algernoon* Sidney's *Sy-
stem of Government, it probably may please any one
that is crept into the same discontented Republican
Party, but what he says is little weight with me, I
shall therefore only make this Observation, that it ,
no disgrace to a Cause, to have an Advocate for a
declared Traitor who suffer'd the Pains of Death
for his Treason, write against it, but it makes for the
Honour of the Proceedings in Parliament, that they
run Counter to* OCEANAS *and Factious* DIS-
COURSES OF GOVERNMENT.

But tho' a part of the Freeholders of *England* cannot impose their Commands on the
Repreſentatives of the Whole, yet may they
repreſent any private or publick Grievance,
nor can I ſee how the doing this can tend
to deſtroy the Conſtitution of *Parliament*. The
Meaning of thoſe who tell us that it does,
muſt be this, that ſome People's complain-
ing in behalf of the Publick, may probably influence others and thus occaſion *Petitions* from all
Parts of the Kingdom What if it ſhou'd do ſo ?
What if far the greater part of the Freemen
and Freeholders of *England* ſhou'd ſend *Petitions,* and repreſent publick Grievances ; how
can this tend to deſtroy the Conſtitution of Parliament ? If there be any Law which forbids the
People to addreſs, or give any Inſtructions to
their Delegates, the doing ſo muſt be own'd to
be againſt Law, but tis not a Treſpaſs, which
(to ſpeak in the Phraſe of a certain Patriot) can
pull up a Conſtitution by the Roots

Anſw. If a Part of the Freeholders of *England* can not impoſe their Commands on the Repreſentatives of the whole, *why ſhould not the*
                                              County

County of Kent *fall under the Houſe's Diſpleaſure for Attempting it, and if they Repreſent Grievances by way of Upbraiding their Superiors for not Redreſſing 'em, where is the Infringment of the Liberties of the Subject if they are Puniſhed for ſo doing? But here were no ſuch things as Grievances laid before 'em, they wanted a War that others might be Aggrieved, and were wearied with a Peace, that had kept 'em ſomething more Honeſt than ordinary for three whole Years.*

But we are told, that by the Conſtitution of our Parliament, the Members are left to the Freedom of their own Debates, and are to act without Controul, they therefore who take upon them to intermeddle in their Buſineſs, invade that Freedom, and conſequently our Conſtitution They who tell us that the Repreſentatives of the Freemen of *England* have ſuch a Freedom as this, and are to act without Controul, cannot ſure mean that they have delegated their whole Power to them, ſo that 'tis free for them to do whatever they pleaſe, without any regard to the Inclinations or Intereſt of thoſe who employ them. 'Tis not to be ſuppos'd that he who takes what Servant he pleaſes, is oblig'd to ſuffer him to do what he pleaſes. The Knights, Citizens, and Burgeſſes, ſent by the People of *England* to ſerve in Parliament, have a Truſt repoſed in them, which if they ſhould manifeſtly betray, the People, in whom the Power is more perfectly and fully than in their Delegates, muſt have a Right to help and preſerve themſelves. Were not this ſo, the Condition of thoſe who act by De'egates, would be worſe, and their Freedom leſs than that of other States; which I think is not ſo in the reckoning of Mankind

Anſw. *The Knights, Citizens and Burgeſſes, are ſent by the People of* England *to ſecure the*

I

Liberties in Parliament, and take care that the respe-
ctive Places they are chosen for do not suffer in the
Loss of their Immunities, or for want of a due Regard
to their Customs and Priviledges. They are a sort of
Champions that undertake our Defence, and espouse
our Cause, and are as much Superior to those they
assist with their Councils, &c. *as he that makes the*
Law is to him that is directed by it, or a Person
protected *to him that give's him* Protection, *and*
whatever may be meant by calling them the Peoples
Servants, *'tis certain they are* the Peoples Masters
by their own Act and Choice, and may keep 'em under
such Rules of Government as seem most adviseable
to the guidance of right Reason, and the direction
of Wisdom and Justice

The *Achaians, Etolians, Latins, Samnites,* and
Tuscans, formerly did, as now the United Provinces of the *Netherlands,* the *Switfers,* and *Gri-*
sons do, transact all things relating to their Asso-
ciations by Delegates, The *Athenians, Cartha-*
genians, and *Romans* kept, as the *Venetians, Ge-*
noeses, and *Lucchefes* do now, the Power in their
own hands. These all, as the above-nam'd Honourable Author observes, were and are equally
free. But 'twould, I think, be very improper
to reckon them so, unless we suppos'd that the
Power committed to their *Trustees* remain'd still
in them.

Answ. A Free State (*as I take it*) *is a sort of*
a Commonwealth that is not Govern'd by a King, but
is rul'd by Laws that are not Monarchical. such as
Hamburgh *and other* Hans Towns, *and was what*
Mr Sidney *drove at in his pestilent Schemes re-*
lating to Government. *Wherefore the Authorities*
he makes use of from the abovemention'd Author
are not pertinent to the Business in Hand, since they
are recited to Justify what they were not written in
vindication of, and are brought in to Assert what
was never intended by them.

That

That the Power arifes and is fix'd here, and
that the Delegates reckon themfelves oblig'd
to follow the Directions of thofe who chufe
them, is evident from the practice of other
Countries, whofe Governments had the fame O-
rigin with that of *England.* The Deputies or
Procuradores of the feveral Parts of *Caftile,* did
in the *Cortez* held at *Madrid,* in the beginning
of *Charles* the Fifth's Reign, excufe themfelves
from giving the Supplys he defir'd, becaufe they
had receiv'd no Orders in that Particular from
the Towns that fent them ; and afterwards receiving exprefs Orders not to do it, they gave
His Majefty a flat denial. The like was frequently done during the Reigns of that Great Prince,
and of his Son *Philip* the Second The fame
way was taken in *France,* as long as there were
any General Affemblies of Eftates, and if it do
not ftill continue, 'tis becaufe there are none.
For no Man who underftood the Affairs of that
Kingdom, did ever deny, that the Deputies were
oblig'd to follow the Orders of thofe who fent
them.

*Anfw. If I chufe a Perfon for my Commiffioner
in any Affair, and refign up the management of my
Intereft entirely to his difcretion, I inveft him with
the Power I had of doing Juftice to my felf, and
have it no longer in my Breaft to propofe terms of
Agreement, &c I muft ftand by his Decifion in
the matter, and hold my felf contented with whatfoever Judgment he fhall make. I may indeed lay
forth the hardfhip of my Cafe, and propofe it to
his Confideration, but I cannot enforce him to act
altogether in my favour, and without any regard
to Impartiality, decide the matter he is entrufted
with, to my Advantage. The fame may be done by
Countys and Burroughs at the Choice of their Reprefentatives, who may be reminded of the feveral Grievances the refpective Corporations lie under ;
but*

but not by way of Command to redrefs e'm, but by way of entreaty, and in a dutiful manner that becomes Supplicants to petition *for Favours they ftand in need of.*

In the General Affembly of Eftates held at *Bloys* in the time of *Henry* the Thiid, *Bodin,* then Deputy for the Third Eftate of *Vermandois,* by their particular Order, propos'd fo many things as took up a good part of their time. Other Deputies alledg'd no other Reafon for many things faid and done by them, than that they were commanded fo to do by their Superiors. Thefe General Affemblies being laid afide, the fame Cuftom is ftill ufed in the leffer Affemblies of Eftates in *Langnedoc* and *Brittany* The Deputies cannot, without the infamy of betraying their Truft and fear of Punifhment, recede from the Orders given by their Principals. The fame Method is every day practis'd in the Diets of *Germany;* the Princes and great Lords, who have their places in their own Rights, may do what they pleafe ; but theDeputies of the Cities muft follow fuch Orders as they receive. The Hiftories of *Denmark, Sweden, Poland* and *Bohemia,* teft fy the fame things

Anfw *The General Affembly of Eftates held at* Bloys, *are not govern'd by the fame Laws and Cuftoms as our Parliaments at* Weftminfter, *and in an Abfolute Monarchy as that of* France *is, fhould there be any thing that look'd like Tyranny in the Prince it muft be born with Patience by the People Some Particular grievances in relation to the Corruption of his Officers might be laid forth in all Probability by* Bodin, *but they durft go no higher in* Henry *the 3d's Time , or take the Courage as the Patriots in our Days do of advifing their Prince himfelf, and fearching into the moft fecret Tranfactions of State, for the Security of the People: Their late Conference held with the Houfe of Lords*

*in relation to the Impeachments, gives a noble inſtance
of their Greatneſs of Soul, and ſhews that the Old
Britiſh Courage is reviv'd among 'em, and that
they not only dare to ſtand up for the Rights of the
the Commons, but perſiſt in their Reſolutions of
oppoſing the Deſigns of thoſe whoſe Power in former
Reigns has been ſo exorbitant, as more than once to
have treated* Inferior *Subjeſts like* Slaves, *and
trample under Foot the very Prerogatives of* Princes.

This appears to have been the Conſtitution of
England. Formerly ſays my Lord *Coke, in the
Writs to the Sheriffs for the eleſtion of Commons,
the King ſignified that by the Advice of his Council
he called them together about ſome weighty Affairs,
that concern'd himſelf, the State and Defence of his
Kingdom of* England, *and the H. Church, and re-
ſwred them to chuſe ſuch Men as would promote
thoſe Affairs ; that fer want of ſuch a Power, and
by an improvident Eleſtion, the aforeſaid Buſineſs
might not be left undone* The Buſineſs that requir'd their meeting was publiſh'd in the Writs,
that the Commons and Freemen might conſider
what they thought convenient to have done,
and that they might chuſe proper Delegates, and
direct them as they thought fit. This I take to
be the Reaſon why *'twas always the Cuſtom at
meeting to declare the cauſe of Parliament, which
antient time,* (ſays he) *was ſhew'd in the Chamber de peint, or St* Edward's *Chamber* That
the Perſons elected being more fully inform'd of
the Buſineſs to be tranſacted by them, might
able to give their reſpective Counties timely
information of it, in order to receive their Directions therein. In this Opinion we may be
confirm'd by what that Great Sage of the Law
tells us in another place. · *When any new Device
propos'd on the King's behalf,* ſays he, *the Common may anſwer, That tendred the King's Eſtate,*
and

and they are ready to aid the same, only in this new Device they dare not agree without Conference with their Countries.

Anſw. *My Lord* Coke *in his Inſtitutions by ſaying* formerly *things were manag'd ſo and ſo, does not Affirm matters ought to run in the ſame Channel* now. Formerly *Rebels dar'd Affront the Legiſlative Authority, take Arms againſt their King, and lay violent hands upon God's Anointed; but ſuch Practices are out of door at this time of day, and ought not to be made uſe of as Precedents for tumultuous Proceedings. There is no reaſon becauſe Ruffs and Farthirgals were made uſe of in good* Queen Beſs *her days, that the Ladies ſhould dreſ themſelves after that Antique Faſhion* now. *Our* Edwards *and our* Henrys *had no* Lewis *the 14th to deal with, to oppoſe their Deſigns as ſoon as the were made known to him, and might let the Subject know, by the Writ he was Elected by, what buſineſ was to be done in Parliament, but Times are alter' ſince their days, and Politicks have quite ano he ſort of Appearance. Our Senators are call'd ac by His Majeſty's Writ* ad Conſulendum *in Ardu Regni Negotiis, to conſult about Matters of hi Importance, which are of too great moment to made Publick no otherwiſe than the Commons the ſelves at every Seſſion ſhall think fit.*

Since then in our Conſtitution the Deleg of the People have reckoned that they ha Truſt repos'd in them by thoſe whom they preſented, and that they were oblig'd to m their Will the rule of their Actions, 'twill very hard to conceive how it can tend to ſtroy this *Conſtitution, to pray them to have* gard to the *Voice of the People* If they fail ly diſcharge the Truſt repos d in them by Country, 'twill be impoſſible at any time to cure a Petition ſigned by ſuch a number of (tlemen as thoſe of the County of Kent, v may any ways feem to arraign theii Proceedings; but if their Management bring them under the fufpicion of the Nation, the People, who have a ught to preferve themfelves, muft be allow'd a Libeity, to let them know in civil and refpectful Terms what is the Voice of the People, and what they think the Neceflitys of the Publick. In fuch a cafe 'tis impoffible for all to repiefent the Publick Guievances togethei; fome therefore muft begin, and they who addrefs firft, when there is a good ieafon for it, deferve the Thanks of the Whole. 'Twas impoffible that fuch a confiderable Body of Gentlemen as the *Kentifh* Petitioneis fhould confpire togethei to affront the Houfe of *Commons*; they knew what they did was done in the Eyes and Face of the Nation, that fuch an Act of folly and madnefs muft biing 'em into the loweft degree of Contempt with the People of *England.* They thought therefore what they did was a Duty which they ow'd their Country in that great and nice Juncture; whethei it was fo or no, will appear from

Anfw. The voice *of a Particular Community of* People, *or a felect Body chofen out of a County, muft not be underftood as if the whole Nation joyn'd with them in their defires, or reckon'd the* Voice of the People *in General. Each Particular Member of the Honourable Houfe of Commons has a Truft repos'd in him, for the Prefervation of the Rights which belong to each diftinct* County, City, *or* Buriough, *and if the Inhabitants of the faid Places think themfelves aggriev'd, they ought to 'Addrefs themfelves only to thofe* Knights, Citizens, *or* Burgelles, *they have had the more immediate* Choice *of, not Petition, or (in more adequate Terms) complain againft the whole Houfe for their want of Forecaft, in not preventing thofe Ircoveniencies they fancy themfelves threatned with.* Mr Meredith,

onc

one of the Knights of the Shire for the County of
Kent, told 'em the ill Confequences, and how it
would be refented by the Houfe, nay further, refus'd to deliver the Petition to the Houfe, for fear of
the difpleafure of that Auguft Affembly, and per-
fifted in his Refufal, till he was threaten'd by one of
the Petitioners as a Betrayer of his Country, and
unworthy to be their Reprefentative; and had it been
their Duty to act in fuch a manner, fuch a Confiderable Majority of the Houfe, who had no Perfonal
Enmity againft either of the five Envoys, would
have fcarce concurr'd in the Order for their Imprifonment; and His Majefty himfelf, whofe Juftice even the moft prefumptuous Arrogance cannot
difpute, would never have given Command to have
them ftruck out of the Lieutenancy, and Commiffion
of the Peace, as Mr. Secretary Vernon told the
Houfe he had.

The third and laft Member of this Difcourfe,
which is to fhew what Reafons thofe Gentlemen
had to petition

'Twas notorious to them, and all the World,
that our Affairs were at that time in a very dangerous and melancholy Pofture. They knew
that France has a long time aim'd at the Univerfal Monarchy That as fhe has Maxims in her
Government which are very well calculated for
fuch great Defigns, fo by her carrying on a Ten
years War againft the powerful States confede-
rated againft her, they faw that fhe has Force
to fupport her in her Enterprizes. If her Power was formidable when fhe match'd us only
in her own Strength, it muft be very terrible to
fee her ftrengthen'd with the Union of no lefs a
Power than that, which two Ages before grafp'd
likewife at the Empire of the Univerfe. 'Tis
true indeed, thofe Dominions were not bequeath'd to her, but being given to one of the
Houfe of Bourbon, who muft live under the
Guar-

Guardianfhip, be protected by the Power, and
govern'd by the Councils of *France*, fhe muft
neceffarily and of courfe have the fame command over their Wealth and Force, that fhe had
over her own. This was an early Effect of the
Spaniard's Will ; for tho' in the beginning the
French Party among us endeavour'd to make us
believe, that *France* would be in no better Condition than 'twas before, becaufe the Duke of
Anjou would forget his Father's Houfe, and be
govern'd only by *Spanifh* Councils, yet the contrary was evident at the Time thofe Gentlemen
deliver'd that Petition

Anfw. *Having very methodically confider'd, or
in his own words deliver'd his Opinion concerning the
two firft Parts of the Text that has fall'n under our
Obfervation, he apply's himfelf to make out the Third
with the fame Clearnefs and Perfpicuity of Thought.*
'Twas notorious, *fays he*, to them and the whole
World, *that* France *had a long while aim'd at
the Univerfal Monarchy, &c Why then did not
the whole World rife up in Arms to oppofe it ?
Where was the Neceffity that we alone of all the
Chriftian States fhould firft take an Alarum at her
Defigns, and break thofe Tyes of a perpetual friend-
fhip which we were engag'd in by the late Treaty of
Peace to the moft Chriftian King ? Were we more in
danger than thofe upon the fame Continent with him,
or lefs Powerful to prevent his Defigns than fome
Princes of* Germany, *whofe neareft Concerns was
to make Provifion againft any poffibility of fuch
Enterprizes ? The* Emperor *indeed had fome rea-
fon for making Armaments, and endeavouring to
perfwade other Princes to enter into Alliances with
Him ; He was more immediately related to the late
King of* Spain, *was of a Family which had given
Soveraigns to that Great Monarchy for feveral
Years, and thought himfelf highly injur'd by a Will,
which if genuine, was made againft his Intereft and*

M   *the*

the moft ftri&t Agreements between the moft Ca-
tholick King and himfelf, if fi&titious, was a Viola-
tion of the Right of Kings. But we had nothing to
do with the Quarrel, we were well aſſur'd we had
no Legacies left to us, and no Pretenfions to make on
our Parts, we were fecur'd by our Fleets *which are*
the Bulwarks of the Nation; and the Parliament had
been liberal in building of Ships, and fupplying His
Majeſty to Man the Royal Navy, that tho' it was
not our Bufinefs to begin a Rupture, it was in our
Power to defend our felves, fecure our Navigation,
and Trade, and maintain the Rights of Commerce
with all Parts of the Earth

They faw that the *Milanefe* was deliver'd up
to her; that the ſtrong Holds of the *Spaniſh*
Netherlands, which we have a long time reckon'd the Bulwaik of *England*, and have
fpent vaſt Treafure and Blood to keep them
out of her Hands, were all in the poffeſſion
of her Troops   And not only fo, but that
the Adminiſtration of all the Affairs of *Spain*
were given up to her. Befides this, they faw
how great a Bieach has been made in the Proteſtant Religion fince the beginning of the laſt
Age: That the Kingdom of *Bohemia*, which
was almoſt wholly Proteſtant, is now intirely
Popiſh. That in *Poland*, *Auſtria*, and *Moravia*,
the Proteſtants who were a Moiety of the People, are utterly deſtroy'd. That their Deſtiu-
ction is almoſt compleated in *Hungary* · That
the *Newburgers* from zealous Proteſtants, aie
turn'd deadly Enemies of the Pioteſtant Religion: That the *Palatinates* are wafted with Pei-
fecution, and the *Saxons* their Neighbours are fo
far from being able to fuccour them, that they
are in danger fiom theii own Prince. That in
France wheie they were powerful enough to cai
ry on feveral great Civil Wars ; and in *Piedmon*
where theii Numbeis were much greate* in pio

poition to the Countries; and in *Flanders, Bavaria, Bamburgh, Cologn, Wartzburgh,* and *Worms,* wheie they were very numeious, theii Religion is totally extinguiſh'd.

Anſw. *The* Milaneſe *are ſo far from being poſſeſs'd by the* French, *that they will not as much as permit a* Fiench *Garriſon in any one Place, and the* Capital *of it has lately given ſuch an Anſwer by its Senators to* Prince Vaudemont, *that it will rather be at the Expence of raiſing the* Militia, *than ever it ſhall. It's true indeed, the Town of* Mantua *has a* French *Governour in it, and the Duke of that Name, is apparently in the Intereſts of that Kingdom, that the ſtrong Holds in the* Spaniſh Netheilands, *are Garriſon'd by the moſt Chriſtian King, but his Troops are to withdraw upon his Royal word, as ſoon as the ſaid Towns ſhall be put into a Poſture of Defence, and the* Spaniſh *Army compleated and made Capable of preventing any Inſults on their Frontiers As for the Affairs of Religion, things are in the ſame Condition in* Poland, Auſtiia *and* Moravia, *as they were before His preſent Majeſty King* William's *Acceſſion to the Throne, and ſince no noiſe was made on our ſide in Relation to the Perſecution in the Palatinate before the King* Spain's *Death, why ſhould we bring that in as a Reaſon for War, eſpecially at a Time when it is known that the Elector Palatine has declar'd for his Imperial Majeſty's Intereſt. If he had not forgotten the Diſgrace at the Iſland of* Rhe, *he would never have made mention of the* Proteſtants *in* France, *we have often times attempted their. Relief to our Coſt, and our Enterprizes in Favour of the late* King *of* Bohemia, *have been attended with ſuch a ſeries of Misfortunes and ſuch pernicious Conſequences, that might oblige us to give over our Deſigns of interfering with other Prince's Affairs, and wholly apply our ſelves to our own.*

All

All this was a very melancholy view ; and
that which made it more fo, was to conſider
that *France* (which out of regard to her own
Intereſt, the greateſt and indeed only Obliga
tion in the World to her, was oblig'd by all
means poſſible to deſtroy the Northern Hereſy,
ſhe having made this the Foundation on which
ſhe built her Hopes of Univerſal Monarchy)
was now in a new Friendſhip and Alliance
with the fierceſt Zealots of the Church of
Rome, the *Spaniſh* Clergy, Men whom 'twas
her buſineſs to gratify, and whom ſhe could not
gratify more than by conrriving ſeverer Methods
to torture and deſtroy Hereticks

*Anſw. The Proſpect is Melancholy enough, that's
certain, and we ought to commiſerate the Sufferings
of our fellow Creatures, but did any of the reform'd
Church in* Poland, Auſtria *or* Moravia, *come to
our Aſſiſtance in the many Dangers our Religion has
extricated it ſelf from? Did the* Newburgheis
ſend us any Ships or Forces in the Spaniſh *Invaſion,
or the* Hugenots *in* France *riſe up in Arms when
their King was Arming againſt us, and in conjunction with the late King* James, *was adviſing what
Meaſures to take in order to rob us of our Liberties,
and all that was dear to us? The* Spaniſh *Clergy,
'tis own'd, are great Bigots and Devotees to the
See of* Rome, *but the preſent* French *King is not
ſo dutiful a Son of the Church as to give his Impli-
cit obedience to that Holy Mother. where it is not
for his Intereſts , and ſince there is no* Inquiſition
in France, *and by his own Words,* French *Cuſtoms
are likely to be Introduc'd into* Spain, *in all Probability the* Inquiſitor General *will loſe his Office,
and there will be no ſuch* Court *held in* Philip *the
5th's Dominions. Which ſuppoſition may already
ſeem to be verify'd in the* Inquiſitor General's *being
in Diſgrace at the Court of* Madrid, *for his Confederacy with the Emperor's Party, who is known*

to be the greateſt Bigot to the Romiſh *Superſtition of any Prince in Chriſtendom.*

In ſuch a Juncture as this, 'twas eaſy for a very weak Capacity to ſee what it imported *England* to do in order to ſecure her own and *Europe's* Liberties, and to prevent the utter extirpation of the Proteſtant Religion both at home and abroad. 'Twas evident that *France,* which had made ſuch Advances already, wanted nothing to make ſure of the Univerſal Monarchy, but only to confirm her ſelf in the Dominions of *Spain* ; and as evident it was that every day ſhe continu'd unmoleſted in her new Acquiſitions, her ſtrength muſt grow prodigiouſly, ſo that in a little time it muſt be inſupportable. In that Caſe ſhe had leiſure and opportunity to ſettle her new Dominions, to diſcover the Weakneſſes of their Fortreſſes, as well as Policy, and to repair both ; to learn the Temper of the ſeveral Provinces, and to conſider how they might be ſecur'd, and by what Governours, to make the beſt proviſion that was poſſible for defending *Milan*; and (which has been a long time one of the high Reaches of her Ambition) to get into a quiet poſſeſſion of all the ſtrong Holds in *Flanders.*

Anſw. Weak Capacities generally have the beſt Thoughts of their Abilities, and over-look Difficulties when they would have any Enterprize brought to bear. Any Perſon indeed may ſee things do not ſo well on his ſide, but it's not in every one's Power to remedy what is amiſs Conveniencies are to be laid for, and Opportunities expected, to help forward our Deſigns in hand, and we are not to make uſe of open Violence, till ſuch time as fitting Expedients are found out, which may put us almoſt beyond the poſſibility of miſcarrying Theſe were the prudent Thoughts of thoſe whoſe Wiſdom he upbraids, and tho' France *has had time to provide againſt us*

by

by way of *Precaution*, can *fortifie her Towns
and Garrison, the frontiers which are most expos'd to the Insults of an Enemy*; we have an
*equal Advantage likewise of providing our selves,
and entring into such Negotiations with forreign
Princes in the mean while, as shall totally secure us,
and render us a Match for the most Christian King,
were he never so formidable.*

Besides this, there was another inestima-
ble Benefit which she reap'd by the Quiet that
was indulg'd her. Whilst those who a long time
check'd her growing Greatness, patiently endur'd
this new Union of Power, what could the other
Nations of the World think, but that this uncon-
cernedness proceeded either from an inward Satisfaction that *France* had acquir'd such Power,
or a despair of breaking it, and restoring the Ballance again? The natural Consequence of either
Reflection must be to resolve that 'twas their Interest to submit, and indeed to make their Court
to a Power which was likely to meet with no
opposition.

Answ. *France had arm'd her self under the
Pretext of making good the Treaty of Partition,
had Troops almost innumerable, ready to take th[e]
Field upon the first Occasion, and was in a Condition at the Decease of K. Charles the 2d o[f]
Spain, to have done what she pleas'd, in spight
of all the Force of* Europe, *then in being: Th[e]
Motion of the* Germans *is naturally slow, an[d]
requires Time to be perform'd in ; the* Italia[n]
*Princes were in general averse to a War, or
had introduc'd too much Luxury into their sever[al]
States, to recover their old Martial Temper whic[h]
they were once Famous for; and the* Dutch we[re]
*so unprovided in their Frontiers against such
rest Neighbours as compass'd 'em on every sid[e]
t ... Declaration of War, had been an em[i]*

L

Loſs of the Liberty's of Europe, *which in all pro-*
bability may be preſerv'd by the prudent meaſures
that have lately been taken Cunctando reſtituit
Rem, *was the Character of a* Roman *General,*
by a Cautious delay he reſtor'd Rome *to her for-*
mer Greatneſs, and made amends for the raſh
and precipitate Conduct of thoſe that had almoſt
ruin'd her, and who knows but our late Proceed-
ings may deſerve the ſame Praiſe, *ſince it is not*
much to be fear'd but they will be attended with
the ſame Succeſs.

'Twas this that made the *Spaniards*, and the
People of their Provinces tamely ſuffer one
of the Houſe of *Bourbon* which they hated,
to take poſſeſſion of their Dominions 'Twas
this made other States enter into Neutralities and
Alliances, which they would have refus'd, had
not the quiet and peaceable Conduct of others
govern'd their Inclinations. Having once fix'd
their Reſolutions, 'tis to be fear'd we ſhall find
them adhere too obſtinately to what they have
ingag'd to *France*, and reſolv'd with themſelves
If honour be not ſufficient to influence them,
and keep them ſteddy to the Side they have
choſen, even Intereſt may help to do it now;
for the Notions of that alter, when Men have
new modell'd their Thoughts, and let their
Heads run upon other Schemes

Anſw. *The Treaty of Partition in all Appear-*
ance, not our unprovided State, made the Spaniards
take ſuch Meaſures as they did, and occaſi n'd
the WILL in favour of the Houſe of Bourbon,
and our adhering to too precipitate Counſels, broke
off that Confidence which was mutually entertain'd
between th two Nations What r is therefore
the Fault of the Miniſtry, ought not to be imput-
ed to the Parliamen , who to their after g Honour
h ve

have Impeach'd the Projectors of that ignominous Treaty as ENEMIES TO THE PUBLICK GOOD, and great Contributors towards the Exorbitant Greatness of France. *They gave away those Kingdoms which these would keep in their due Obeaience to* Spain, *and parcell'd our Large Tracts of Land to the Family of* Bourbon, *when it's as certain as truth it self from the Publick Votes, that these have Address'd His Majesty to enter into a strict Alliance with the House of* Austria, *and other Confederate States in order to oppose the Possession of what they so easily made a Grant of.*

In that great Juncture, when the Season was for making the earliest and best provision for securing the Liberties of *Europe,* the Eyes of the World were all fix'd upon *England.* 'Twas she who had always kept the Ballance; and she only having it now in her power to determine whether it should be preserv'd or no, other Nations were to observe her Motions, and take their Measures from her. None could doubt but that if she had enter'd betimes into a firm League with the *Emperor* and *Holland,* 'twould have presently produced a Confederacy strong enough to humble *France,* which was grasping at things much beyond the reach of her Power, in that feeble and weak Condition she was reduc'd to by a long War and evil Conduct.

Answ. *At the Death of the King of* Spain, *the Eyes of the World were fix'd upon* England, *in order to know how they would relish such a Disposition that was made against the Interest of her Antient Confederates. But the Constitution of this Kingdom would not allow of such Measures as the Pamphleteer would have us take at*

the

the very receipt of the News. His Majesty indeed might have declar'd a War as it was part of the Royal Prerogative, but he could not carry it on successfully without the Consent of his People, the Sinews of it were wanting, Funds already given for the Service of the Publick Deficient, and the Nation nigh Twenty Millions in Debt. When the Parliament sat, they acted so cordially for the Preservation of the Peace at the same time as they were employed in finding out Ways and Means to begin a War, that whoever will take the pains to examine their Proceedings, must needs conclude they have done as much for the People of England as ever their Representatives did, and have studied the welfare of our Antient Allies, as heartily as ever Men did.

'Twas therefore undoubtedly the Business of *English* Ministers to advise the calling of a Parliament immediately upon the news of the *Spaniard*'s Death, and of the Parliament to address the King to make *Alliances* Had this been done *Portugal* would have thought it her interest rather to enter into Alliances with them, than make her self a Party in establishing the Throne of the Duke of *Anjou*, who when he is establish'd and made one with *France*, will certainly set up his Title to *Portugal* The Duke of *Savoy* then would have consider'd that it was by means of the *Equilibrium* between the House of *Austria* and *France* that his Ancestors preserv'd their Dominions; he would have consider'd likewise whether 'twas worth his while to make his Sons Beggars, or Soldiers of Fortune, for the sake of aggrandizing his Daughter This will be the Acquisition of his Battles if they be successful; for when the *Milanese*, and both the *Sicilys* are in the hands of France, his Dominions will be necessary to her for Communication

Answ.

Anſw. *What was the Effect of* Evil and Corrupt Miniſters Advice, *ought not to be imputed to the
Conduct of thoſe that have arraign'd 'em for want of
a due Forecaſt, or (what is worſe) a ſtock of Ho-
neſty, but ſhould be laid at the doors of the Contriv-
ers. However the Parliament might have been call'd
together before the* Middle of February, *and yet the
King of* Portugal *would not have reſiſted the Offers
of* France *which were ſo much to his Advantage,
and bound* Spain *to , elinquiſh her Right and Title
for Ever to the* Luſitanian *Provinces , The Duke cf*
Savoy *likewiſe was too nearly related to the* French
*by the Marriage of one of his Daughters to the
Duke of* Burgundy, *and more entirely devoted to
his Intereſt by the Promiſe he made that the other
ſhould be Queen of* Spain, *and tho' the* Equilibrium *between the two Powerful Houſes of* Auſtria
and Bourbon *made his* Anceſtors *preſerve their*
Dominions, *the Advantagious Propoſals made to
him on the Parts of* Lewis *the* 14th, *and* Philip
the 5th, *made him certain of adding freſh Titles to
his Family, and being the moſt conſiderable Prince
in all* Italy.

The Pope then probably would have reflected
on the Affair of the *Corſi*, the Extention of the
Regale, the four Propoſitions that were advanc'd
at *Paris*, and all the enormous Attempts againſt
the Dignity of the Head of the Church in the
Perſon of Pope *Innocent* XI. and would perhap
have declar'd for the Emperor, had he had ſuch
encouragement to do it. Nor is it improbable
that the Republick of *Venice* would do the ſame
ſhe could hardly avoid conſidering betimes, tha
the Neighbourhood of *France* prov'd ſo fatal t
her in the ſmall number of Years that *Lewis* XII
enjoy'd *Milan*, that he reduc'd her to greater Ex
tremities than any other War, even that of th
Turks, ever did. A Conſideration ſo powerf
with that wiſe Republick, that tho' the va
Pow

Powei of the Houſe of *Auſtria* undei the Em-
peioi *Charles* V· might have given her juſt
grounds of jealouſy, ſhe would never lend her
Eai to any Piopoſition of *Francis* I. Succeſſoi
to *Lewis* XII.

Anſw *The* Pope *would ſcarce haʋe turn'd*
Proteſtant, *and join'd with* England *and* Holland, *from the Specimen he has already given of
the bent of his Inclinations for the* Piopagation *of
the* Romiſh *Faith, and the valuable Preſents he has
made towards the* Support *of the late King, as
well as Promiſes of contributing what lies in his
Power towards His Reſtoration.* The Buſineſs *of
the* Regale *cannot well be digeſted by one of his
Cholerick Temper, and the* Ioui *propoſitions,
doubtleſs, ſtick in the holy Pontiff's Stomach, however he has been hitheito ſo far from ſhewing his
Reſentments, that he has in a maι ner own'd the New
King of* Spain, *by permitting Him the* Nomination
to vacant Biſhopiicks and Abbys ; *and the Republick of* Venice *ſeem inclinable to the* French
*Intereſt, in adhering to a ſtriſt Neutrality, even
at a Time when the* Geiman Foices *are ſo powerful and triumphant in the very Heart of* Italy, *as
to Countenance their pulling off the Mask, if they
had any Intentions to befriend 'em.*

Had things been upon a right foot in *England,* 'tis veiy piobable that the Duke of *Bavaria,* and his Brothei the Arch-biſhop of *Cologn,* would have iemembred the Obligations
laid upon them, at leaſt their own Intereſt ; and
that the foimei would have taken Meaſuies which
would make the Wai much eaſiei than 'twill be.
In thit Caſe the People of *Spain,* and their Provinces, would, if they did no moie, keep up
their old Reſentments againſt *France,* which in
a convenient Seaſon would iender them veiy
uſeful to the Confedeiate⸗

Anſ.

*Anſw. When Princes have Ingratitude in their
very Natures, it muſt ſhew it ſelf at the firſt Opportunity* The *Duke* of Bavaria *owes his Government of the* Netherlands *to K.* William's *Intereſt
with the late King of* Spain, *and his Brother the
Electorate of* Cologn *and Principality of* Liege, *to
his Wiſe Negotiations: But neither the Obligations
which were laid upon the One, in the Proviſion for
the Succeſſion of his Son, the Electoral Prince to
the whole* Spaniſh *Dominions, nor the Friendſhip
which was ſhewn to the Other carry'd that Weight
with em as they deſerv'd The latter of theſe two
Prince s Territories lie ſo much expos'd to* France
and Spain, *and the firſt has ſo many Millions due
from his late Catholick Majeſty for his Salary, and
what he has laid out in defence of the* Spaniſh Netherlands, *that he m ſt run the riſque of every
Floin the* French *King ſtands engag'd ſo the
Payment of, ſhould he take other Meaſures Since
the Emperor is not in a Capacity to reimburſe it to
Him. and His Majeſty is ſo uncertain of puſhing
on his Conqueſts over all* Spain, *that tis to be
doubted whether he can get ſo much as footing in
the Dukedom of* Milan*

The *Germans* would conſider what danger
they were in of having a Prince, grown
ſo great by the Acceſſion of the *Spaniſh* Dominions, carry his Arms into *Germany* where
he has great footing already, and challenge
all the States that compoſe that great Nation as part of the Succeſſion of *Charlemagn,* of
which he and other Kings of *France* have already declar'd themſelves Heirs In this Caſe ſome
(as the Chapter of *Cologn* ſeems very lately to
have done) would conſider that in an Hereditar-
ry Empire, there would be no more Colleges,
nor Diets nor Chapters Others, that 'tis a vain
thing to diſpute about Prerogatives, and to make
France judge of the Diſpute, whoſe Arbitration
                                                        muſt

muſt turn to the Ruin of the Empire. And the reſult of theſe Reflections would be to enter into Meaſures agreeable to them.

Anſw. *The* Germans *would ſtill have been the ſame ſlow Creatures, as they are at this Juncture, and would not have brought their Troops into the Field before it was time to ſhut up the Campaign, and march back again into Winter Quarters. Their ſwiftneſs in proſecuting Affairs, and ſtanding up for the Intereſt of the* Empire, *may be ſeen from the haſt they have lately made to aſſemble together for one anothers mutual Defence, and their ſuffering the* French *to have an Army that Conſiſts of more than fifty Thouſand effective Men, when they have not ſo much as five Thouſand drawn together to oppoſe their Deſigns.*

Theſe probably had been the Reſolutions of thoſe Foreign States, at leaſt of ſome of them, had not the management of *England* diſcouragʼd them to that degree, that they muſt arraign themſelves of raſhneſs and folly, if they had taken thoſe Meaſures which they themſelves knew were moſt for their Intereſt.

Anſw. *The* Management of England *has been ſuch, that the States of* Europe *that are Afraid of a French Yoke, muſt needs be encouragʼd to contribute what lies in their Power towards the Advancement of the Publick ſafety from it. The* King *declares from his own Royal Mouth, that nothing can more effectually conduce to our Security, than the unanimity and Vigour which the Commons have ſhewʼd in this laſt Seſſion. But this Author contradicts his own Soveraign, and affirms that is is too late, and would make the World believe that they are been negligent of our Security, and that of our Proteſtant Neighbours? Whom we ought to give credit to, Manners will direct us, and His Majeſtys words without doubt have more weight with the wiſing Part of the Nations, than the Expreſſions*

of

of a Party that never acted any thing yet that was
Confiderate.

Things being in this ftate, 'tis very plain that
the Gentlemen of *Kent* had a great deal of rea.
fon to pray the H--fe of Com--ns to have a Regard *to the Voice of the People, that our Religion*
and Safety might be effectually provided for, and
that His Majefty by *Supplys* might be *enabled to*
affift his Allies. The *Voice of the People* was then
every where loud for War, there was fcarce any
fo weak as that they could not fee that no Provifion could be made for our *Religion* or *Safety*
without it. 'Twas manifeft that *France,* after
fhe had been a while fettled in her new Dominions, would be able to overcome *Holland* whene-
ver fhe pleas'd. *Holland* being overun, 'twas
eafy to fee that *England* being fpoil'd of her
Trade by that Revolution, and the Union of the
two great Kingdoms, muft foon follow her Fate.

Anfw. *But fuppofe things are in a qu te differem*
State (as certainly they are) and bear another fort
of Face than what he puts upon 'em The Voice
of the People *will foon drown the* Voice of a
few *Kentifh* Men, *and fend forth other Clamors*
than what are made ufe of to call for frefh Defola-
t ons, and fupplicate for an Addition to thofe Mif-
fortunes which are but too preffing upon us already.
Poverty difplays it felf to a great degree in all our
Borders. and the Tears of Widows for their flaugh-
ter'd Husbands, and Children for their deceaf
Fathers are not yet dry'd up. Should we therefo.
be fond of having a new ftream burft forth for
our Fellow Subjects Eyes, or lavifhly call for a new
ftock of Miferies by petitioning for a War to re-
reduce 'em? Should we feek for the fare Cau
which have occafiond thefe deplorable Effects?

The *French* Party indeed told us, and (whic
a mong other things occafioned fome Reflect ors
the H--fe of Com--ns feem'd to fome to be
                                                  the

then Opinion, that our Security might be fufficiently provided for by a good Fleet. 'Twas a very fond Opinion to imagine that we, who in conjunction with *Holland*, were the laſt War infulted upon our own Coaſts by the Fleet of *France*, and another time had probably been ruin'd by them, had not the Heavens been favourabe to us, fhould be able, after the loſs both of our Trade, and the Affiſtance of the *Dutch*, to maintain a Fleet big enough to fecure us from a Power fo exorbitant as that of *France* would then be A Powerful Fleet are words that found plaufibly in the Mouths of thofe People, who are for having our Arms to be as little grievous as may be to *France*, and they ferve to amufe and impofe upon weak People; but Men of underſtanding muſt allow this to be a very uncertain Security.

Anſw. *We were never worſted in our Fleet joyn'd with that of the* Dutch, *by the* French, *and what he calls inſulting us upon our own Coaſts, was after the Engagement of forty two* Engliſh *and* Dutch *Ships with all the Naval Strength that belong'd to* France. *That miſcarriage laid at ſome Great Mens Doors, who were then Commiſſioners of the Admiralty, not in the Fleets of either* England *and* Holland, *and 'tis Apparent by the little uſe the Monſieur* Tourvill *made of that Engagement, that he had other thoughts of our Strength, and the Conduct which has been ſhewn by* Lewis *the* 14th's *Admirals ſince, is a Token enough of their diſtruſt of their own Power, rather than a Confidence they have of its being Superiour to Ours, and we are capable at this Time without the Affiſtance of the* Dutch *to Equip two Hundred Sail of Veſſels of War to Sea, in order to our further ſecurity, which is wholy owing to the Conduct of our Parliaments that have rais'd ſuch vaſt Sums of Money to build 'em for the Preſervation of theſe Kingdoms*

This

This was the only Provifion for our Safe
ty, which the Parliament for a long time
feem'd inclin'd to allow us. Whatever matter was offer'd that feem'd to have the leaft
tendency to a War, was violently oppos'd by the
*Sp--er, Mu—ve, Scy--r, Sho--r, Fi--ch, H--w,
Ha--rt*, and all thofe who were entuely in the
Intereft of that Party. This Averfion they
plainly difcover'd in the beginning of the Seffion, when on the 14*th* of *February*, immediately after the King had made his Speech, they
came to the Refolution, *To ftand by and fuppor-
His Majefty's Government, and take fuch effectual
Meafures as may beft conduce to the Intereft and
Safety of* England, *the prefervation of the Proteftant Religion, AND THE PEACE OF EUROPE.*
We cannot but remember what Debates arofe
upon this laft Claufe, and with what Difficulty
'twas carried by 181 againft 163, and that the
Reafon why 'twas oppos'd was, becaufe 'twas
plainly declaring for a War. Here it was that
the Prejudices began againft that Party in the
H--fe, and this laid the Foundation for the
great fufpicions that follow d afterwards.

 Anfw. *The moft weighty Confiderations induc'd
thofe Gentlemen to think, that in fo great and important an Affair, as the Bufinefs of War, they
could not act with too much Caution: They confider'd 'twas an eafy thing to have recourfe to Arms,
but the difficulty was to obtain fuch a*Peace *by the ufe
of 'em, as to enable 'em to lay 'em down with Honour and Advantage to the* Englifh *Nation. They
could not but take notice of the forwardnefs of thofe
Gentlemen to enter into a new War, who had got
moft by the management of the Laft, and took it as
a great difcouragement to Honeft Country Gentlemen to fee the Nation fo much in Debt, and the
Chief Managers of Publick Affairs fo vaftly Rich.
And therefore fince the Circumftances of the King-*

*dom were such, that they were not able to do in this
as in the* laſt *War, ſince the Emperor was the Principal Party concern'd, and the* Dutch *in more immediate danger, the Commons thought it very rea-
ſonable, that thoſe two Powers which were chiefly
aggriev'd ſhould make the firſt advance towards it,
and in Caſe an Honourable Peace could not be at-
tain'd, the Empire and* Holland *ſhould apply themſelves to* England, *and not* England *to them. That
is, they were not againſt bearing the greateſt Bur-
then of it, as they did in the* Laſt. *For had they
declar'd at the beginning of the Seſſion what they
did at the latter End of it,* Holland *had been o-
ver-run, the* Dutch *ſurpriz'd, all the* Engliſh
and Dutch *Merchants Effects ſeiz'd abroad, and*
England *it ſelf almoſt in Danger of an Invaſion.*

'Twas amazing to all thoſe who could diſcover
no poſſible means to preſerve us, but by a vigorous War, to ſee ſuch a great number of the Repreſentatives of the Freemen of *England,* labour-
ing for that which of all things in the World
France moſt deſir'd, and would give any Money
for. Nor was this the Voice of that Party in
the H--ſe alone, but all without Doors who
were of their Faction, and all who had any byaſs
to *France,* or St *Germain* Family, were every
where induſtrious and noiſy in decrying a War,
and ſetting forth the inconveniences of it. But
that which gave the melancholieſt Reflection of
all, was to find that thoſe who were thought to
have the ſole Direction of publick Affairs, were
in the ſame ſentiments. They ſpoke their Minds
freely upon that Subject, as we have been told,
ſo did their Friends; and the ſaying of one Gentleman in great Station, to C--t *Vra--au* the
Em---r's Min--er, ought to be remember'd.

*Anſw. So amazing as it was, the moſt conſide-
rate Part of the Houſe of Commons, as well as
thoſe that had any Stock of* Intellectuals *in the*

O   *Natio.*

Nation were for taking such measures as to pre-serve the Peace of Europe without entring into a War, and keeping the Ballance in its due Poize, without making use of such Means as certainly would incline it to the French *Interest. The most Christian King had not such a Distrust of His own Strength, nor such an ill Opinion of above Two hundred thousand compleat Troops, and as well re-gulated as any in Christendom, that he stood in fear of any Insults whatsoever, but was willing to see his Grandson not mount His Throne from Heaps of slaughter'd Carcasses, or swim to the Possession of Both* Indies *thro' a Sea of Blood, and tho' 'tis well known He might have acted on the offensive Part, and been very Troublesome to some Neigh-bours, He made it His Choice to wait the Motions of those he had Reasons to call Enemies, and stood prepar'd only to resist Force by Force, should any be so hardy as to attack him. Since therefore he was Powerful and strongly provided with such nume-rous Armies, those cannot be thought to be Friends to* France, *that took time to put themselves like-wise in a Posture of Defence, that endeavour'd to oppose His Designs without a Declaration of War, and made Armaments by Sea and Land, in hopes that the report of their Strength might induce him to stand by the Peace, in surrendring up such Cautio-nary Places to* England *and* Holland, *as should be agreed on by the Parties concern'd.*

What then Sense was, the Author of the three *Essays* told us before the Parliament sat; the manner of his expressing it speaks it to be publish'd with their Allowance, and those who know his Conversation with them, were per-suaded it was. " If any among us (*says he*) " seem at present willing to embrace peaceful " Councils, and to declare entering upon im- " mediate Action; 'tis not that they doubt " themselves, or dread the adverse Strength, or
" that

" that their antient Enmity to *France* is buried in
" Oblivion. --They are not fo apprehenfive of
" Coping with any foreign Strength, as they are
" fearful they fhall be compell'd to enter into
" frefh Confliéts with the Enemies of *ENG-*
" *LAND,* whom they had almoft fubdu'd, &c.
" Their Ears can never endure the Cries of the
" Poor. for want of Work, &c 'Tis a mon-
ftrous *Tenderrefs and Compaffion,* which can endure rather to fee Popery and Slavery difplay
their Banners in this Land, than to behold the
Calamities which a new War muft bring upon
their Country. If he can fee how they can be
kept out without a War, he fees things in quite
another Light than what any honeft Englifhman
does

Anfw *A Gentleman in a great Station who muft
need: be a Privy Councellor at leaft, world fcarce drop
any word that fhould let Count Uiatiflaw know that
the Bent of the Court was not for a War, and if
the Author would reflect with himfelf who got Mo-
rey the laft War, and heap'd up confiderable Treafures, who manag'd the Funds that were given
for the Publick Security, for their own Private
Intereft, and occafion'd fuch a Deficiency in 'em,
as is now but too vifible, he would fcarce bring them
in for Sticklers againft it Befides, His Majefty
their Mafter's Martial Genius, His averfion to the
French Intereft, and his defire to bring down her
growing Greatnefs, are fuch convincing Arguments
for thofe that are in Places under him to be of the
fame Sentiments, not to enter into Difcourfe with the
Emperor's Minifter that fhould be fo unpleafant to
him, and which he could not but expect would come
to the King his Mafter s Far, who had efpous'd the
Auftrian Family s Intereft. As for Dr. Dave-
nant's Book, the Arguments of it are of fuch
weight with all thinking People, and the Reafons for
a Peace fo poignant and ftrong, that if the Houfe*

O 2   *did*

did actually allow he spoke their Senfe, *they muft needs acknowledge he ha, done 'em all imaginable Juftice in expreffing it*

One would think he thought but flightly of a War, when he tells us, that one of the greateft things to be dreaded in it is, that 'twill bring thofe Men into play again, who never gave us the leaft fufpicion of their being in any other Intereft than that of their Country 'Tis very eafy to perceive what his Defigns are, both in running down thofe Men, and labouring to give us a difmal Idea of a War But he and his Friends tell us, that his Book fhews him to be plainly for a War. 'Twas cunning in him to fay fomething, for fear of falling under the rage of an injured Nation ; and 'twas Policy to grant him a Difpenfation to do it, left by being too plain in handling an odious Subject, he might put it out of his Power to do any Service for the future. He feems fometimes to write for a War, but (which fhew'd his Inclination) voted a- gainft it amongft the 161 he ought indeed, l e faid, to do otherwife, but *Ja--k H--w* fmil'd fo pleafantly upon him, that he could not divide againft him

Anfw. If 'tis the Intereft *of the* People *of En- gland to have the Publick Treafures exhaufted, and thofe entrufted with the care of it that were of flen- de- Fortunes, and confequently would endeavour to raife themfelves by the fingering it ; if they acted for their Countries good that poftpon'd every other Confideration to their own enrichment, end like a cer- tain Pay-mafter, that tells the* Publick *Money o- ver a* Grid-Iron, *and challenge's all for his own that fall's thro' it, got incredible Eftates from ve- ry fmall Beginnings, then the D: is infallibly in the Wrong But, if it be not fitting that thofe who have been guilty of fuch Male-Adminiftration, fhould be brought into the Miniftry again, if the*

Id a

Idea of the War is difmal *enough of its own na-*
ture, more efpecially when that Nutriment that
fhould feed it, and thofe Funds that are the Sinews
of it, are made over to other Purpofes, where are
the Effays upon the Ballance of Power *to be*
found fault with, that State the Cafe as it really is,
and give us fo clear an infight into the Mifcarria-
ges that are likely to attend too precipitate Confulta-
tions ? He lays down the Reafons both for and a-
gainft a War fo clearly, and handles it with that
fincerity of Judgment, that he leaves the Reader
wholy to determine which is moft advifeable in our
prefent Condition, and a Gentleman of his known
Integrity and Senfe, that has refus'd feveral Offers
to engage with another Party, *in any underftanding*
Man's Opinion cannot be thought to be prevail'd on
by a Smile, *efpecially when Mr.* How's *Reafons are*
well known to be more Cogent than his Looks.

When he fpeaks for a War, 'tis very cold-
ly, and in other Places he takes care to
deftroy the Force of what he faid ; in one place
he tells us " That we reap little from a War but
" the Perils and Loffes with which it is like to be
" attended. This is but a fmall Encouragement to it In another he is afraid " fuch a
" Debt will be at laft Contracted, *and moft of*
" *it abroad,* as in time muft impoverifh and fink
England. What then muft we do? Why, " all
" Englifhmen ought ferioufly to confider this
" Reflection which *MACCHIAVEL* makes,
" That when a Prince, or Commonwealth, ar-
" rives at that height of Reputation, that no
" Neighbour, Prince, or People, dares venture
" to invade him (unlefs compell'd by indifpen-
" fable Neceffity) he may do what he pleafes.
" In all probability, *fays he,* The *French* are
" now arriv'd to this formidable pitch of Great-
" nefs, unlefs the *Spaniards* fhew more Courage
" than has appear'd in any Meafures they have
" taken thefe laft hundred Years. Anf.

Anſw *A Perſon that writes impartially, muſt as well ſhew the Difficulty of an Enterprize, and point out the Misfortunes that may caſually attend it, as buoy up his Reader's Imagination with the hope of Succeſs; and if the Dr. tells us* we can Reap little by a War, &c. *it's no more than what is viſible to any Man of Senſe. ſince we have no Pretenſions on our own Parts, either upon* France *and* Spain, *and whatever Articles are concluded on between the Emperor,* France, *and* Holland, *as the Reſult of a War, it is to be feared, neither* Oſtend *or* Newport *will fall into our Hands, any more than the Sea Town of* Carthagena, *ſince we have much the ſame Right and Title to the Mines of* Peru *and* Mexico, *as we have to any individual ſtrong Hold in* Flanders. *As for the* French *Greatneſs, I preſume, we can ſay no long to detract from it, and I muſt agree with the Dr. that unleſs the* Spaniards *revive that Courage which has been in ſo long a ſtate of Declenſion, that their Antient Monarchy's Grandeur will be forgotten and ſwallowed up in the Glory of that which has now furniſh d it with a Prince, that cannot make it Greater than the Kingdom he drew his firſt Breath* in.

If this be ſo, that the Power of the *French* is grown too great to be reſiſted, and we have no hopes but from the *Spaniards* taking good Meaſures, we are in a very miſerable Condition. But Lord, he ſhews us ſom hopes yet, " It they can ſo prevail, as t " make their young Prince become a goc " *Spaniard*; if they can divide him from *I* " Councils, --- if the quiet Reception he is li " to find make *French* Councils, and *French* S " ports no longer neceſſary to him, thoſe ſea " will be ſomewhat allay d, which we now l " bour under. But are there any hopes th 'twill be ſo Yes ſure, very great; " Hc giv " us promiſing Hopes of his Perſon, and not " man

martial young Prince, if he be endow'd with
' any fhare of his Grandfather's Conduct and
' Wifdom, may put *Spain* into a better Condition
' than it has lately been, to oppofe *France* in
" any Attempts it may hereafter make upon
" the Liberties of *Europe*.

And w Either the Spaniards *muft take mea-
fures difagreeable to the* French *Intereſt, or the
Imperors Army in* Italy *is not likely to make very
Succeſful Campaigns, or keep Garrifon in the
Caftle of* Milan *, and if they can't prevail with
their young Prince to become a* Good Spaniard, *'tis
very probable he will be accounted an* Excellent
French *nan. It is our Bufineſs therefore undoubtedly, not to fall out with him, but fince we have
Recogniz'd his Acceffion to the Throne, to live in
Amity and a good Underftanding with him, that
he may not be forc'd to put his whole Dominions under the Protection of* France, *and furrender up
the Nethe lands to his Grandfather and his Heirs
for ever by a* Treaty of Partition, *which would
be very difagreeable to* England *and* Holland, *in
order to preferve the reft of that vaft Monarchy
to himfelf.*

O wonderful Contrivance to ferve his Mafters
and perfuade *England* to lay afide all thoughts of
War ! Could he expect to do it by fuch little
fetches as thefe, to fcare a great and warlike People with his paltry reprefentations of the Power
of *France*? Or to lull a wife Nation afleep with
fuch a filly profpect of Security ? Yet this is one
of the great Machins which C---t *Tal---rd* the
chief *Fr----ch* Engineer in *England* has made ufe
of, not only to bomb great Minifters, and every
thing he has a mind to reduce to Afhes, but to
batter down all the ftrong Holds ard Fort.effes
of our Religion and Liberties This is he that

is carefs'd by great Men of our own Court; this
is he that is employ'd to *teach young Gentlemen the*
Bufinefs of the Nation; who is to tell them in
print a little before the Seffion begins, what they
are to do the next Seffion. If this be our Condition, that the weighty Affairs of the Kingdom muft be manag'd by Senators, who are to
learn their Wifdom from fuch a Wretch as this,
in Charity we ought to pray for them, in the
Language of our Saviour, *Forgive them, for they*
know not what they do ; but for our felves, in thofe
which we write over the Doors of Peft-houfes,
Lord have Mercy upon us.

Anfw. *Now the Man of Argument is fallen*
into a downright Rapture, and is troubled with an
Oratorical fit by way of Exclamation! The Dr.
faid, the young King of *Spain* gives us pro-
mifing hopes of his Perfon, *&c. and may*
learn from his Grandfather's Politicks how to Op-
pofe France *in any Attempts on the Liberties of*
Europe. *Where is the harm in thefe Expreffi-*
ons, thou great Lover of Interjections ; that art
mov'd by fuch a fudden Paffion of the Mind?
Does an Ambitious King mind the Ties of Blood,
or Obligations of Kindred? Will a Prince that
rules over a Jealous turbulent, and Proud Peo-
ple as the Spaniards *are, fo far endanger the*
Lofs of his Crown, as to act contrary to the Sen-
timents of his Subjects. Have not they been bred
up in an Averfion to the French *Nation, and al-*
moft fworn at the Altars in their very Infancy
as Hannibal *againft* Rome, *to maintain a per-*
petual Enmity with 'em. Are not they at this
time uneafy at the Conduct of the Regency that
have permitted fo many French *Gentlemen to*
attend their King, and will they ever fhake off
thefe

their Refentments for fome indignities lately of-
fer'd by them to the Natives? 'Tis *impoffib'e they*
muft lofe their very Natures before they can part
with their Hatred; and if the Dr is Ca eß d by
great Men of the Court, its ce tainly a fi n that
he cannot be in the Intereft of France, *or King*
Will. *muft have a very Treacherous Min ft y*

If he, who in times of the greateft Danger,
when it moft nearly concern'd *Fr--ce* to try the
power of her Gold here in *England*, has been highly courted by her *Tal---rd*, and given very g eat
demonftrations of his Zeal to gratify the Ambition of that K ngdom, can make himfelf and Intereft, not only to be protected in his Infolencies,
but to be courted like wife by a Party, and befides
all this, to have the Honour confer'd upon him,
of being made the Leader of the Blind, 'tis eafy
to fee what in a fhort time muft be our Doom :
that between the Management and Conduct of
Men of too much Intreague, and too little Underftanding, we muft fall under the Dominion
of *French* Tyranny and Popery

Anfw. An Ingenious Man will be carefs'd *by*
Men of all Perfuafions and Count Tallard *was*
fuch a Judge of Converfation, that he could not mifs
him amongft the reft of thofe Polite Gentlemen *he*
made his Court to, and if to difcourfe with a French
Minifter, or fit at Table *with him, is a Token of be-*
ing Brib'd *by him, we have feveral* Noble Peers,
and amongft them great Officers of State that have
fpent an Evening with his late Excellency, and have
certainly been Partakers of his Largeffes.. But with-
out doubt our prefent Miniftry is of another ftamp,
and the Gentlemen in it are too well fatisfy'd with
their Places of Honour and Profit, *to contribute any*
thing towards the fupport of an Intereft that is contra-
ry to theirs; and the Dr is Remarkable for fuch a
Love to the welfare of his Country, and fuch an ear-
neft defire for its Profperity, that he is ready to fore-
go any mercenary Advantage whatever, and prefer

is

*its Consideration to all things that are accounted va-
luable.*

This the *Kentish* Gentlemen thought they
had Reason to fear, would be the Effect
of the Measures taken by our Parliament, before they offer'd their Petition. To descend
to the particulars of their Proceedings, which
brought them under the so universal Censure
and Displeasure of the People, would be too
invidious an Undertaking, and raise this little
Discourse to a much greater bulk than I design'd. My Intention is only to shew, that the
Gentlemen had Reasons to offer their Petition at that time. If one or two good ones
are sufficient to justify them, and they may
be taken notice of without any great Offence,
I must desire my Reader to rest satisfied with
my mentioning them. Matters that are nicer
and not so well bear touching, I leave to be
handled by Men of more Penetration, whose
Fears (I will not say Concern) for the Publick
are greater perhaps than mine are.

Answ. *Popery and Slavery have been at too great
a distance from* Kent. *or any other Part of the Kingdom for these twelve Years last past, to make the subject apprehensive of any ill Effects from it. And his
Reasons must be better than any he has given yet to
perswade us to believe that his five WORTHIES fears
had any grounds for 'em, at least such as deserve to
be handled by an* Abler *Pen than his own, that has
such a mighty concern for the security of the Publick.*

If those Petitioners were really perswaded that
Fr---ch Gold had any influence in the management
of Publick Affairs, 'twas a sufficient Reason for
them to endeavour by such a Petition, either to
make the *Ho--se* of *Com--* take other Measures, or
to dispose the other parts of the Kingdom to follow their Example. That they were of this
Perswasion, we have very good Reasons to believe. We know what one of the five Gentlemen

en said in a very publick Place, some Weeks
fore the Petition was offer'd, to Sir *Fr---cis*
---la, a Member of Parliament, concern-
g the Inclination of the *Ho--se* of *Com-
-ns* to serve the *Fr---ch* K---g. 'Tis not pro-
able that that Gentleman would have been so
bold to speak openly, to a Member who was en-
irely in the Interest of that Party which he
suspected, words which the other call'd *Seditious*,
if he had not reckon'd it a Service to owd his
Country, in a very great and dangerous Crisis
Answ. *A Man cannot be really perswaded of the
truth of a Matter, unless he satisfies himself from O-
cular Demonstration, or other indubitable Proofs;
therefore the Kentish Petitioners must either a-
ctually have seen Count* Tallard *distributing his French
Gold, or recc.v'd the Truth of it from unquestionable
Authority, or according to their Advocate's own Argument which is a convertible Proposition, their Petition
must be groundless, and 'tis not be suppos'd but any
one of that Company which had Forehead enough to
behave themselves so Irreverently to the whole Body of
Parliament, would not stick to affront Sir* Francis
Child *who was only a single Member of the House.*

About the time they petition'd, this suspicion
was grown so universal, that what a Gentleman
told Sir *Ed---rd Sey---r* in *Hampshire*, near the
time the Parliament rose, that *we were bought
and sold*, was the Voice of the People every
where. This Jealousy must run very high, and
there must sure be very good grounds for it,
when a very great Lord could say, in a very August Assembly, just two days after that Petition
was deliver'd, that so me things that were done,
shew'd that there was *Fr---ch* Money in the Case

Answ. *Without doubt Sir* Edward Seymour *return'd a suitable Answer to the* Hampshire *Gentleman, and was not wanting in his vindication of that
House he had the Honour to be a Member of* and
what a Great Lord said in a very August Assembly

w is

was spoken in relation to other Peoples being suspect
of Bribery not the House of Commons whose Hono
be has the highest Deference for.

But this was not all. Those Gentlemen saw
as I observ'd before, that not only all the leading
Men of that Party, which bore sway in the
Ho---se of Com---ns, but some leading Men i
the Nation likewise, us'd all possible endeavour
to drive People from the thoughts of War. Th
those Gentlemen, and the bulk of the Peopl
thought the greatest Service that could be don
to *Fr---ce,* and that the certain consequence o
that would be, that in a little time we must b
content with what Religion, what Liberty, anc
what Trade *Fr---ce* would be pleas'd to allow
us. This being then sense of things, 'twas
sufficient Reason for them to do what they did

Answ. *He has already prov'd the Kentish Gentle-*
men's sight was not good, because they could see no-
thing at all of the Matter, but took it upon Hearsay
and yet he dwells upon the Commendation of the clear-
ness of their Forecast, and brings in the Bulk of the
People, *that is the whole to Justify what was done at*
a Goal delivery, *and vindicate what neither the*
Bench of Justices could add a sanction to by their sub-
scriptions, or the Wiseacres their Impertinent Deputy
by their Imprudent behaviour at the Bar of the House
of Commons

What a happy Nation should we be, if others
would imitate them in their Zeal, and virtuous
Concern for the Publick! Now is the time for
Englishmen to shew themselves. Things are
brought to the highest Crisis that ever was seen
in *Europe* *Fr---ce* plainly designs the Universal
Monarchy. 'T s War only that can determine,
whet'er she shall have it or no, If she prevail,
our Fate is manifest we must come under the
Dominion of *French* Popery and Tyranny. If
i e miscarry, the Misery and Devastation which
she

fhe will bring into her Kingdom, will be greater than, perhaps, fhe may be ever able to furmount In this Cafe *England* will not only continue in Poffeffion of her Religion and Liberties, but become the greateft Nation in the Weftern World. What our Fate fhall be, depends upon our Management now.

Anf. *What a fenfelefs Nation fhould we be, fhould other Countys imitate their follys, and take a Pattern from their unadvis'd Conduct ! What an unhappy State would the People of* England *labour under, fhould they take the fame Refolutions to Affront their Superiors, and fall out with thofe Patriots that have done as much for the Prefervation of thefe Realms, as ever Parliament did or People could expect ! Our Alliances are maintain'd, Our Fleets are out at Sea, Payment is taken care of for the Publick Debts, and Parliamentary engagements to the lafting Honour of this Seffion are once more accounted facred. What could be the done on the Part of the* Subject, *or hop'd for to the Affiftance of the* Prince ?

'Tis plain, that without a War we are undone, fo we may with it, if thofe who have the Management of Publick Affairs, fhould happen to be in the Intereft of the abdicated Family, or common Enemy, or fhould be under the old Prejudices againft the *Dutch,* which were in the late Reigns. We know what fufpicions we have had, and what grounds there were for them, this makes it abfolutely neceffary, that the Nation reprefent it felf anew. 'Twould be very furprifing to fee the prefent *Par---nt* fit again, when a great Party in it has given fuch Umbrage to the Nation ; when they were thought (as far as it was poffible for them to venture, without plainly difcovering themfelves, and becoming too notorious) to do all that *Fr---ce* could defire to have done. If then Conduct throughout the Seffion was fuch as made it evident, that their Addrefs to the King, towards the latter end,

was

was only defign'd to prevent their Diffolution, or fecure their Election if they fhould be Dif-folv'd; 'twould be as ftrange to fee this Par---m continue, as 'twill be to fee fome chofen a-gain, if it fhould be diffolv'd 'Tis upon that Election the Fate of *England* depend : if care be taken to chufe Perfons, who love our prefent Proteftant Settlement, and have no manner of Byafs to *France*, or the Abdicated Family, no-thing can prevent the Ruin of *France*, and *England*'s being made a great and flourifhing King-dom.

Anfw. 'Twould be very furprifing therefore fhould His Majefty give Ear to fome Ill difpos'd Peoples Advice, and diffolve that Parliament that has fhewn fuch Loyalty to his facred Perfon, fuch an Affection for his Confederates, and fuch a Zeal for the Pro-teftant Intereft both at Home and Abroad, that no Seffion can Parallel More Money has indeed been rais'd in the LateWar, but never more in time of Peace when fo many Debts were left unpay'd by the precedent Parliaments, and fo many Incumbrances on the Publick Faith, fo that it is not to be doubted, but the fame King that has been fupported by 'em fhould ask Advice of the fame Councillors, and that Princes who promis'd to meet 'em again in Parliament next Winter, and gave 'em fuch inftances of his Satisfaction in his Speech at their laft Prorogation, will continue the ferfe he has of their good Services, and have a relyance on their Fidelity fo far as to be in a farther condition of returning 'em thanks again for what they fhall do for him.

APPENDIX.

1. A Lift of fuch Members of this prefent H—— of Com——, as refus'd the Voluntary Aſſociation in 1695.

SIR J--es Eth——dge.
Ld. H——de.
t- n M——ſt——n.
H——y Fl——ng.
t——n Tr——m.
?——s Gw——n.
Anth- ny H——nd
ſir E——d S ——ur.
J--n Gr——il.
Th——s Str——ys.
Th---s F——ke of Dorſ.
R——d F——nds.
J--n H——w.
R——d H——w
Th--s Br——ton.
P——r Sh——ly.
ſir J--n B ——lles.
G——rt D——en.
ſir R——it J——ſon.

H——ry F——nch.
Sir E---d N——rus.
Th---s R——ley.
J——mes B——rty.
J--n K——ſton.
Sir J -n Tr——an.
H——ry H——mes.
Su J--n L——ſon G--re
Su H---ry G——gh.
J---n L——knor.
W---m Br——ley.
F,——s Gr——il.
Sir Ch---r M——ʒt.
R---rt B——rty.
W——m H——vey.
H---ry P——ntl
S---l S——ft
R——t B——ley.
Sir J---ry J——iys.
Sir J--n C——ay

B. Names

B. Names of the Perſons Committed by the *H---ſe* of *Com---ṇ* this Seſſion.

To the Tower.
{ JOHN *Parkhurſt*, Eſq;
John Paſchal Eſq
William Coteſworth, Eſq;
Samuel Shepherd, Eſq; }

To the Gate-houſe.
{ Mr. *William Colepeper.*
Mr *Thomas Colepeper.*
Mr. *David Polhill*
Mr. *Juſtinian Champneyes.*
Mr. *William Hamilton.* }
{ Theſe were taken into Cuſtody of the *Serjeant at Arms*, and after ſent to the *Gate-houſe.* }

To New-gate.
{ Mr. *Laurence.*
Mr. *Glover.* }

Taken into the Cuſto-dy of the Serjeant at Arms.
{ Mr *Edward Martyn,*
Mr *John Dunmal*
Mr. *Clayton.*
Mr. *Perks*
Mr. *Story.*
Mr *Jeffreys.*
Mr. *Bourman.*
Mr. *Maſon.*
Mr- *John Newark.*
Mr *Marſh.*
Mr. *Branſby.*
Charlwood Lawton, Eſq,.
Mr. *Alexander Cutting.* }

Mr *William Adye.*
Mr- *Edw. Allen.*
Mr. *Julius Samborne.*
Mr. *Joſeph Whimbleton*
Mr. *Warham.*
Mr. *John Hayſham.*
Mr *William Clifton.*
Mr. *Edward Whitacre*
Mr. *John Whitbrough.*
Mr *James Buckly*, Jun.
Charles Maſon, Eſq;
Mr *James Buckly*, Sen.
Thomas Terry.

F I N I S.

Lightning Source UK Ltd.
Milton Keynes UK
UKHW050706260720
367133UK00004BA/134

9 781385 275